DATE DUE

FE 03 '00			
AP 26 '02			
GAYLORD			PRINTED IN U.S.A.

THE PEACE CORPS
AND PAX AMERICANA

THE PEACE CORPS
AND PAX AMERICANA

By Marshall Windmiller

Professor of International Relations
San Francisco State College

Public Affairs Press, Washington, D. C.

309.2

PREFACE

Like that of most Americans, my reaction to the creation of the Peace Corps was a very positive one. It seemed to me to combine idealism and practicality in a way that no other government agency had ever been able to do. I was therefore pleased when I had an opportunity to participate in the Peace Corps training programs that were undertaken at San Francisco State College. My role in training volunteers was essentially limited to lecturing on world affairs and leading seminar meetings, but it gave me an opportunity to meet a number of volunteers and Peace Corps officials. In general, they made a good impression on me, and I became a booster of the Peace Corps to my students, many of whom subsequently became Volunteers. I also supported it in public lectures and on my weekly radio program.

In the fall of 1965 opposition to the Peace Corps appeared on the Berkeley campus of the University of California, a school which had been the source of a large number of Volunteers. The leader of this opposition was Professor Gerald Berreman, an anthropologist and one of the faculty members most active in protesting the war in Vietnam. Berreman argued that students and faculty who opposed the war should do so by withholding services from the U. S. government, particularly those agencies like the Peace Corps that are involved in foreign policy.

I disagreed with Berreman. While I was equally opposed to the war, and while in general I agreed with the idea of withholding services from the government, I continued to make an exception of the Peace Corps. There was so little that was imaginative and idealistic in the U. S. government, that I was reluctant to oppose the one agency that seemed to promise something new and different. I hoped that the Peace

Corps would be a progressive bridgehead into an otherwise stultified foreign policy establishment, and that in time it would stimulate some basic changes.

I held to this position for two years, but my doubts grew constantly. They were fed by the mounting evidence of the subversive roles being played in developing nations by the CIA and the Green Berets. The United States was attempting to police the world to protect its interests and to establish a sort of Pax Americana over the third world. It was a policy without legal or moral justification. Vietnam was powerful evidence that it was also destined to fail, and, in the process, damage American democracy at home. The Peace Corps could not be regarded as separate from that policy. It was, in fact, one of its most effective instruments.

This is not to say that the Peace Corps is a police force or that Volunteers are engaged in law enforcement. However, their role may be analagous to that of the community relations divisions found in some of the major metropolitan police departments. The men of these organizations serve as a buffer between the police and the community. They try to ease tensions and prevent outbreaks that might require the use of force. They are, in a sense, public relations men who try to create a good image for the authorities.

The more I examine the Peace Corps, the more it seems that its essential role is this kind of public relations work in behalf of American power and influence in the developing world. The Peace Corps is making Pax Americana seem legitimate and benevolent when in fact it is neither. While this is not the conscious intent of most volunteers, it is nevertheless the effect of what they are doing. It is counterinsurgency in a velvet glove.

In my judgment, American policy toward the developing world has become patently exploitative and therefore cannot be legitimized. By 1967 my early hopes that the Peace Corps would become something other than an instrument of public relations for that policy were dissipated. In November of that year I devoted a radio commentary to this subject and called upon young people to withhold services from the Peace Corps. The broadcast script was reprinted in the underground press, circulated informally by photocopy within the Peace Corps and reprinted in at least one Peace Corps newspaper. It stirred some controversy. Professor Berreman then wrote an article, "The Peace Corps: A Dream Betrayed," for the February 26, 1968 issue of the *Nation*. These criticisms so disturbed the Peace Corps that Washington sent an official to Berkeley to refute them and to engage Berreman and myself in debate. It was during the ensuing dialogue that I decided to write this book.

The Peace Corps was the novel creation of John F. Kennedy and bears the imprint of his style and philosophy perhaps more than any other artifact of his presidency. This book deals primarily with the development of the Corps under Kennedy and how it evolved under President Johnson, for it was during this period that its role as an instrument of U. S. foreign policy was most subtle and therefore most effective. Under President Nixon there is no fundamental alteration of the philosophy, but the style is different, more obvious, and less likely to be misunderstood.

The analysis given in this book requires some background concerning the expansion abroad of U. S. business. I have tried to supply this in brief form, especially in Chapter II. The most obvious way to document this phenomenon is to cite directly what its practitioners say about it, and for that reason I have used extensive quotations from the publications of government, the business community, and its supporters. These quotes are the hard, essential evidence. They speak for themselves more eloquently and authoritatively than dry statistics or academic analyses.

The main reason I think this book is necessary is that the Peace Corps is made up of many fine people. Because of this, it is hard for most Americans to believe that they could be doing anything that is not constructive. When one thinks of expansionists, imperialists, and conquerors, one does not have in mind well-scrubbed, idealistic young people who want to teach English and mathematics or dig tube wells. That such people could be important agents of expansionism doesn't seem plausible. Yet history provides evidence that the most decent and generous people may be the most vigorous expansionists. That is what I think the Peace Corps Volunteers are today. A growing number of them now realize it; it is time the rest abandon their innocence.

Many people have helped me in gathering material for this book and in reading and criticizing the manuscript. I wish to express my appreciation to them all. Any errors of fact or interpretation are, of course, my responsibility.

MARSHALL WINDMILLER

San Francisco State College

CONTENTS

I: THE ARGUMENT

"... When you are hungry, you may have our game. You may gather our sweet fruits. We will give you food when you come to our land. We will show you the springs, and you may drink; the water is good. ... We will be friends; and when you come we will be glad.

"We are very poor. Look at our women and children; they are naked. We have no horses; we climb the rocks and our feet are sore. We live among rocks, and they yield little fruit and many thorns. When the cold moon comes, our children are hungry. We have not much to give; you must not think us mean.

"We are ignorant—like little children in understanding compared with you. When we do wrong, do not get mad, and be like children too. When white men kill our people, we kill them. Then they kill more of us. It is not good. We hear that the white men are a great number. When they stop killing us, there will be no Indian left to bury the dead ..."

Statement of a Shivwits Paiute Chief in council with Mormon explorers in Colorado, 1870.

Since its beginning, the Peace Corps has had a good image. "From the front porches of the U.S.," said *Time* magazine in 1963, "the view of the Peace Corps is beautiful. The image is that of a battalion of cheery, crew-cut kids who two years ago hopped off their drugstore stools and hurried out around the world to wage peace."

The public image of the Peace Corps is that of an experiment in practical altruism—a people-to-people effort aimed at fighting hunger, poverty, ignorance, and disease. According to this image, sedulously fostered by the Peace Corps itself, the Corps is not political, and it is not an instrument of American foreign policy. "In the American mind," said Associate Director, Harris Wofford, "it took its place somewhere between the boy scouts and motherhood."

In this book, I shall show that this image is grossly misleading, that the Peace Corps is highly political and that it *is* an instrument of American foreign policy. I shall attempt

1

to show that the predominant characteristic of American foreign policy is expansionism, and that the essential role of the
Peace Corps is to aid and abet that expansionism.

In making this argument, I wish to emphasize certain qualifications. One has to do with expansionism, about which
people hold strong feelings linked to words and phrases like
"conquest", "domination", "imperialism", "satellites",
"hegemony", and "spheres of influence". While in general
I disapprove of the expansion of the power of the strong
over the weak, I think it must be noted that expansionism is
not always totally evil. The strong sometimes bring benefits
to the weak whom they dominate. Whether these benefits adequately compensate for what amounts to the expatriation of
sovereignty depends upon one's values, point of view, and
the particular case.

The Peace Corps is a mitigating factor in American expansionism, bringing some important benefits to those peoples
who are being prepared for, or accustomed to, American
influence and control. But this mitigating quality actually
reinforces and accelerates the expansionism by diluting, co-
opting, and disarming opposition to it. I shall attempt to illu-
minate this phenomenon by comparing the Peace Corps to an
historical model, the relatively enlightened administrative
approach of the British Raj in India.

Another qualification to the basic argument relates to the
motives and intent of the Peace Corps administrators and
volunteers. I am not suggesting that they all approve of
American foreign policy, or that they are conscious participants in a master plan of American expansionism. Many of
them would argue from sincere, albeit ill-informed, conviction, that the United States is not expansionist. Many are
devoted altruists, and many even disapprove of American
foreign policy. Moreover, I doubt that a master plan of
American expansionism exists. I see no grand conspiracy,

although the activities of the Pentagon, the CIA, and some academicians suggest at times a network of minor interlocking conspiracies. The relationship of Michigan State University to the CIA in bolstering the Diem regime in South Vietnam is one example. But what is more important is an apparent national missionary zeal based on self-interest and considerable self-delusion. Americans seem to have a great talent for helping themselves while sincerely believing that their aim is to help others.

While American expansionism has given many benefits to the world, it is, in my opinion, on balance, a danger to peace and freedom. This is true because it exhibits greediness, cruelty, and most important, a lack of concern for legal norms. Whether in Vietnam, Cuba, Bolivia, or the Dominican Republic, the dominant operational philosophy of American foreign policy is that might makes right. The coupling of this philosophy with unsurpassed and aggressively employed technological prowess presents a danger to all hopes of establishing an orderly world in which the powerful, as well as the weak, are subject to the restraints of enforceable law.

I set forth these judgments about American expansionism in order to make my opinions and biases clear. I believe they can be fully documented, and I have provided considerable evidence in Chapter II. To go into greater detail would blur the focus of this book, which is the Peace Corps, and is unnecessary given the extensive treatment by other writers.[1] I also believe it is unnecessary to detail the reasons for my opposition, on similar grounds, to the foreign policies of the Soviet Union, China and other world powers although perhaps some readers ought to be assured that I do not condone or take lightly the dangers they present to the peace of the world.

I recognize that many will regard American expansionism as a benevolent force, and from that perspective will welcome the Peace Corps' role in it. This book is not addressed to them and will not persuade them otherwise. But many more will simply deny that it exists or that it is in any way analogous to imperialism. I hope that they will find in these pages new information and stimulus to thought.

The Peace Corps presents a dilemma to men concerned with moral values in an imperfect world. For example, should a young man or woman join the Peace Corps in the hope of helping poor people who need his or her help, or should they reject the Peace Corps because by joining it they become agents of U.S. foreign policy, aiding and abetting American expansionism? The message of this book is that given existing U.S. foreign policies, given the urgency of domestic, economic, social, and political reform, they should reject the Peace Corps. Should these factors change, I might argue for a different answer, but the highest priority is to change them. In the hope that eventually they will change, I have set forth in the conclusions some ideas about a better Peace Corps.

One way of thinking about political power is to divide it into two kinds: the power to destroy, and the power to build. Both are necessary in order to bring about fundamental political and social improvement. The power to destroy is by far the easiest to acquire and develop, for it requires little self-discipline and less intellect. Young people around the world today are developing great amounts of such power. They do not appear to be creating proportionate amounts of the power to build. The Peace Corps is an exception to this phenomenon. The Peace Corps as an organization, and most volunteers as individuals, seem to me to be builders by temperament and intellectual commitment. They constitute, therefore, a group of great potential worth in the reconstruction of American society. It is in the hope that this potential will soon be fully utilized that I feel justified in drawing attention to the way that it has been misused.

II: U.S. EXPANSIONISM

"The Peace Corps represents the best in the American ideal because it helps the peoples of the world follow the American example of peacefully reordering their society within the philosophical concept that man is capable of determining his destiny.

"The Peace Corps is a reflection of our diverse, pluralistic society. The peoples of Latin America, Africa, and Asia see young men and women of different color, different religious faiths, different economic and social backgrounds and different geographic and cultural heritages, leave our shores with a common purpose—that somehow Americans must help the less fortunate of the world attain a higher degree of human dignity. To do less would be a travesty of the American ideal of which I speak today.

"We must encourage this great work, not because the program must be sold. The Peace Corps is already sold to more American volunteers than the Peace Corps can train, and to more interested countries than the Peace Corps can supply with volunteers. In a word, the program can stand on its own merits and on its own record of success. The question before us is are we willing to permit the Peace Corps to carry out the historic mandate of the American tradition of helping others secure human dignity."

Rep. William F. Ryan, Nov. 13, 1963.

There is an official catechism about imperialism which has been generally accepted by Americans without criticism since the 1940's. It was stated rather succinctly by Under Secretary of State Douglas Dillon in a speech in Chicago on October 2, 1960. "Imperialism," said Dillon, "is an old problem. But all reasonable men recognize that nineteenth century colonialism has outlived its day and is fast disappearing. . . . While the colonialism of the Western European powers is steadily and surely making way for independence, the reverse process has been ruthlessly put into operation within the Soviet bloc by the Soviet Communist party. Today, the world is confronted by a new kind of imperialism—Soviet Communist imperialism—which is more comprehensive and more infamous than anything mankind has ever known."

Dillon argued that Khrushchev's doctrine of peaceful co-existence was really an instrument of imperialism. "The Soviet imperialists speak of 'peaceful coexistence'," said Dillon. "It is important that this jargon be translated into words that ordinary men can understand. The actual meaning is relatively simple: it is the slogan under which these twentieth-century imperialists aim to conquer the world without risking general war. They utilize economic pressure, political infiltration, and civil disturbances."

The propaganda battle during the Cold War between the Soviet Union and the United States was largely a contest to see which side could pin this dreaded label of "imperialism" on the other. There were good reasons for such a serious struggle over a word, for this word has acquired great power during the last fifty years. Not only has it satisfied masses of uneducated colonial people as a single, simple explanation of their misery, it has also acquired intellectual force with the writings of J. A. Hobson, V. I. Lenin, and others.[1]

While the propaganda battle was waged among the nations, anti-Communist intellectuals in the West mobilized not only to demolish Hobson and Lenin in particular, but to discredit economic interpretations of imperialism in general. In the United States this effort was largely successful, perhaps as much because of the atmosphere of McCarthyism as due to the intellectual merit of the critique. In the 1950's there were few academicians who were willing publicly to defend a theory that looked like Lenin's. A major triumph of the anti-Communists was that imperialism came to be perceived in the United States as a process of military conquest resulting in colonies or satellites. The idea of Hobson and Lenin that imperialism really began with the export of capital, particularly its investment in backward countries, was generally considered as discredited, and certainly beyond the pale for respectable academicians. It is still difficult in academic circles to raise questions about the relationship of economics to foreign wars without having a colleague point out that this is "the classical Marxist-Leninist analysis" and therefore unworthy of serious rebuttal.

One measure of the extent to which economic theories of imperialism and war causation have been discredited in the United States is the frankness with which the business community and its press have discussed the extent of American investment overseas. Perhaps the outstanding example of this frankness is the article in *Nation's Business* for February 1968, entitled "When the War Ends: A World of Opportunities." Here are some excerpts:

"The best thinkers on the subject in business and government agree that magnificent business opportunities await in Viet Nam, Thailand, Laos, Indonesia, Malaysia and Singapore. As the military situation in Viet Nam improves, they expect the flow of business to double, triple and quadruple.

"There are dark spots and danger areas, of course, but nothing is foreseen that would keep Southeast Asia from becoming an industrial business outpost of the first water. . . . Many well-known American businesses are in Southeast Asia, even in Viet Nam—Bank of America and Chase Manhattan Bank, Foremost Dairies, Caltex, Esso, American Trading Company, Landis Brothers and Co., Inc., Brownell Lane Engineering Co., American Chemical and Drug Co., . . .

"But that's only a handful compared to the number that could be there, Agency for International Development people insist, especially in view of the protection provided for American investments and the concessions offered by Southeast Asian governments to get foreign business.

"Herbert Salzman, a former business man who is now Assistant Administrator for Private Resources for AID, says: '. . . The U.S. government encourages business by eliminating some of the risks. . . .

" 'In Southeast Asia there is a tremendous surge in purchasing power as a direct and indirect effect of the U.S. presence.

" 'This creates markets and an effective demand for products, many of which could and should come from the United States. . . .'

"The American businessman moving into the Viet Nam market is protected 100 per cent by the federal government against expropriation, inconvertibility of currency and war risk. He is protected up to 75 per cent of his debt capital on extended risk, including commercial risk, and 50 per cent of his equity investment.

"Another incentive provided by the federal government allows a company to go into a high risk foreign country like Viet Nam on a management contract with little initial investment. It also provides the opportunity to buy into the foreign company later.

"If he decides to make a prior survey of his business chances in Viet Nam and subsequently finds the market not worth the candle, AID pays half of his expenses. This includes costs the businessman incurred in sending representatives abroad, their hotel, food and incidental expenses.

"The Rand Corp. has gone into the prospects of getting profits out of Viet Nam and says: 'Many of the new industrial investment projects launched within the past five years experienced rates of return of the order of 20 to 40 per cent; and capital recovery in two or three years has not been unusual.'

"American business methods are showing up in all-Viet companies. They have completely replaced French and traditional Vietnamese methods.

"American businesses being established in Viet Nam, through investments, acquisitions, partnerships or subsidiaries, will find an expanding network of communications, highways, waterways, docks and airports, every one of which could be useful to industry or commerce.

"In the past few years, six new deepwater ports have been built, eight shallow draft ports, eight jet air bases with 12 new 10,000-foot runways, 80 smaller fields, scores of bridges and hundreds of miles of roads, oil tanks and pipelines, storage and maintenance facilities and housing for 325,000 soldiers, much of it convertible into housing for industrial workers.

"Each month thousands of Vietnamese receive industrial and business training, either elementary or advanced, and they go into a manpower pool which can be useful to American private business someday. . . .

"Viet Nam is beyond doubt one of the prime investment points for American know-how in Southeast Asia. But there are others.

"*Thailand*—This is one of the most promising underdeveloped nations in the world. . . . The government is dictatorial but it is effective and stable and so is the economy. GNP goes up 7.3 per cent yearly. . . .

"Among the best bets for success are businesses involving agriculture, fertilizers, cotton processing, manufacturing, zinc and tin mining, tourism. . . .

"*Indonesia*—This can be the great sleeper for U.S. business. . . . Many an American business expropriated by Sukarno is being restored. A half dozen of the largest U.S. chemical and mining companies are either setting up operations in Indonesia or completing feasibility studies which generally indicate the country is worthwhile as an investment site. Four American banks have recently moved in.

"Best bets are in minerals, forest products, oil, tourism, manufacturing, agriculture and agri-business.

"*Malaysia and Singapore*— . . . Malaysia is an excellent place for private investments. There is a good investment law and Malaysian money is strong. GNP goes up six per cent yearly. A large bond issue was recently floated on the New York market.

"Several American companies have moved into a new industrial park near Kuala Lumpur. Three American banks have branches in the country along with American chemical companies, paper manufacturers and agri-business concerns. . . ."

The pro-business *Time* magazine (March 19, 1965) carried a similar article about opportunities in Latin America. It said in part:

"A worldly group of businessmen gathered in Buenos Aires last week to speak of Latin American investment in an unaccustomed atmosphere of hope. Eighty-five bankers and industrialists dedicated to bringing together U.S. investment dollars and Latin American opportunities, had come from every part of the hemisphere for the annual meeting of the Inter-American Council of Commerce and Production. This year the meeting was more important than usual: after several years of growing disenchantment, U.S. investors are again showing interest in putting money into Latin America. . . . New U.S. investment rose from $64 million in 1963 to $175 million in the first nine months of last year and is still climbing. . . . The State Department has negotiated detailed agreements with 15 Latin American countries guaranteeing investors against losses from expropriation, currency inconvertibility, war, revolution or insurrection—the very losses that they fear most in Latin America.

"Many American companies have revised their investment plans to include new facilities in Latin America, including Dow Chemical, General Motors and Chrysler, all of which are building large new plants. U.S. Steel, Union Carbide and Alcoa are considering multimillion-dollar expansions there. . . . Venezuela has done such an effective job of mopping up its Communists that Jersey Standard's Creole and other oil companies, which transferred more than $100 million out of the country in 1962 and 1963, are pumping capital back in again. . . ."

In an informative cover story on the Standard Oil Company, *Time*'s issue of December 29, 1967, provided further information on U.S. investment in developing areas:

"Along with sophisticated markets in Europe and Canada . . . globalization is also stretching out to developing markets in Africa, Latin America and the Far East. A total of $11.4 billion has been invested in Latin America, where U.S. companies make and sell everything from automobiles to Mexican peanut butter. Another $10 billion has been committed to Africa and Asia. For example, the Gillette Co., which already controls 60% of the European razor-blade market and which last week also took over the big West German appliance firm of Braun, is now moving in on Africa with its Nacet blades. Gillette offers shaves to Africans who have previously trimmed their whiskers with knives. . . ."

I have quoted these articles at length, articles so commonplace that their significance is often missed, because I believe they make the process of American economic expansionism more understandable than a simple recitation of statistics. They are impressive also because they come from sources sympathetic to this expansionism, and therefore unlikely to present a case biased by commitment to an antibusiness or anti-imperialist position. These articles present economic expansionism as the businessmen themselves see it, and the remarkable thing about it is that they see it in much the same way that Hobson and Lenin saw it, except, of course, that they approve of it, whereas Hobson and Lenin did not.

It is one thing to show, as these articles do, that American investment overseas is increasing, that American companies control important foreign markets, that they contemplate greater expansion, and that the U.S. government encourages them by negotiating favorable concessions and by providing subsidies and guarantees. It is another thing to prove that this is imperialism or that it leads to colonization, or war.

It can be shown, however, that where big American business interests operate in a foreign country, the American government can, and frequently does, exert formidable pressures on its government in behalf of those interests. Here are three examples. The first is a dispatch by Edward Burks in the *New York Times* November 11, 1963:

"BUENOS AIRES, Nov. 10. W. Averell Harriman was understood today to have warned Argentina that her plan to cancel contracts with United States oil companies could sharply impair her prospects for future American help.

"The grave turn in United States-Argentine relations became clear after a series of weekend meetings between the highest officials here and Mr. Harriman, United States Under Secretary of State for Political Affairs.

"Under discussion was Argentina's announced intention to cancel contracts with United States companies, which have more than $300 million tied up in producing oil for the Argentine government. . . .

"One authoritative United States source said:

" 'What the Argentines are going to do I can't tell you. But the American position has been made fully clear to them. They are under no illusions as to the American point of view.' . . ."

The second example is a November 15, 1966 *New York Times* dispatch by Benjamin Welles:

"WASHINGTON, Nov. 14. The United States Government was reported today to be trying behind the scenes to ease the dispute between American oil companies and the Algerian government.

" 'We are bound to try to protect American interests overseas whenever appropriate,' one Government source said.

'The American oil companies have not specifically asked for help so, for the moment, we're urging both sides to settle their differences amicably.'

"Officials here strongly denied allegations of 'pressure' by the American government. The allegation appeared recently in *El Moudjahid*, a semiofficial Algerian newspaper, which said that 200,000 tons of American wheat destined for Algerian relief was being held up until the oil negotiations were concluded to the satisfaction of the American oil concerns. 'This is untrue,' one informant declared. 'The new food-for-peace law was only signed by the President on Sunday and we still have to evaluate the effects of the Findlay Amendment.'

"This amendment, which was sponsored by Representative Paul Findlay, Republican of Illinois, bars food shipments under Public Law 480 to any country that sells or transports goods, strategic or nonstrategic, to North Vietnam. . . ."

The third example also relates to the use of food supplies to apply pressure in behalf of American business. It is a dispatch from the December 20, 1966 *Christian Science Monitor* by Saville R. Davis.

"WASHINGTON. The harrowing struggle between Washington and Delhi over food for India leaves officials and observers here aghast.

"Food pipelines are draining fast, hunger is mounting, and the human drama becomes almost unbearable. Yet the contest of political and economic issues is inhumanly balanced.

"There is reason to hope that an accommodation will be found before the damage becomes too great, either in human or political terms. . . .

"As seen from Washington, the tightening struggle between the two countries—and within each of them—has two major elements:

"1. Fertilizer and the method of producing it. India desperately needs fertilizer on a large scale to solve its own food problem and to end chronic dependence on American food.

"But its nationalized fertilizer plants are yielding disappointingly small output at an agonizingly slow rate, just at the time when the big American oil companies have made very large technical advances and can build plants with 5 to 10 times as much output.

"President Johnson is holding up food shipments, for one reason, trying to induce the Indians to admit the capitalist behemoths. . . .

"The President is seeking, by holding up shipments, to compel other well-to-do Western nations to assume part of the humanitarian burden in India. . . .

"While this hard bargaining drags out, not only are the specter and the fact of hunger on the increase, and the fear of it worsening, but India is aimed for a grave political crisis. . . .

"Mrs. Gandhi has risked her position with the left wing of her party by trying to go along with President Johnson's commonsense approach to the fertilizer problem, though not with the price the oil companies are asking.

"This has alienated some of her socialist followers and outraged others, who argue that the American oil companies have built a reputation as ruthless international bargainers and exploiters. . . .

"Some of the President's advisers . . . echo the Indian complaint that the oil companies are pressing their advantage too far and that the President (with some evidence to the contrary) is not pushing them as hard as he is pushing Mrs. Gandhi toward concessions.

"The opposite, and prevailing, view is taken here by many officials, national and international, and by a quiet but influential minority in Delhi. They say that India will not be persuaded out of its socialist 'inefficiency' in the vital matter of

fertilizer and can only be shocked out of it by superior force
of events and pressures.

"Many Indians confidentially plead with Washington to
force the issue, saying they cannot pay the political cost of
such arguments at home. . . .

". . . sources also say that the American oil companies
face considerable risks in coming into India under present
circumstances and that their profits, while seeming inordinate
to Indians, will be literally small by comparison with the
value of large scale fertilizer and the managerial and technical know-how that India cannot otherwise obtain, to replace
its socialist bureaucracy. . . ."

Each of these three cases was very complicated and it is
not necessary to detail subsequent events. It is difficult to
determine whether American pressure achieved its aims. In
the Algerian case it apparently did not. In the Argentinian
case the Argentinians at first nationalized the oil companies
but subsequently worked out a satisfactory arrangement with
the oil companies after much U.S. government negotiation.
As for India, an interim grain shipment was made early in
1967, and the Indian government announced moderate concessions to foreign investors in the fertilizer industry.
Whether the two events were related is impossible to say for
sure. The point here is not that the American government
always succeeds when it intervenes in behalf of American
business, but that it does intervene frequently and vigorously.

Why does it intervene, and at whose behest? Who pulls
what strings, and how? It is difficult, even for the Congress,
to pry the details out of the State Department. This is illus-
trated by the exchange with took place between Senator
Joseph Clark of Pennsylvania and Lincoln Gordon during
hearings on the latter's nomination to be Assistant Secretary
of State for Inter-American Affairs:

Senator Clark: "Let me ask you specifically whether you

approve of holding up the economic aid to Peru until they make a satisfactory deal with the International Petroleum Corp. which is a subsidiary of the Standard Oil Co. of New Jersey."

Mr. Gordon: ". . . I do not think that that is an accurate characterization of the policy that has been followed because there has been a considerable amount of aid to Peru during the last two years. . . ."

Senator Clark: "It is true, is it not, that our aid to Peru, . . . has been held up pending a settlement, at least in part . . . of this controversy?"

Mr. Gordon: "There have been several AID projects as well."

Senator Clark: "You mean that have been held up?"

Mr. Gordon: "There have been some that have been held up and there have been some that have gone forward. That is a matter which is under very active review at the present time, and I would prefer not to try to state conclusions prematurely." [2]

U.S. government pressures on Peru ultimately produced a reaction by the Peruvian government that was just the reverse of what was desired. On October 9, 1968 it nationalized the International Petroleum Corporation's properties. Peru even commemorated the "Day of National Dignity" with a new postage stamp. Early attempts by President Nixon to secure adequate compensation for the expropriation were a complete failure, and the White House apparently recognized a real danger that the Peruvian case might unleash a continent-wide reaction against American economic interests. It consequently postponed any abrupt public cancellation of aid as required by the famous Hickenlooper Amendment.

There is not only incontrovertible evidence that the American government exerts pressures on foreign governments in order to secure advantages for American companies operating within those countries, there is also evidence to show that the U.S. government uses the companies and the investments to pressure those governments into taking foreign policy positions that they would not otherwise take. Thus American power expands with a kind of push-pull movement: government serves business expansion, and business serves the expansion of government power.

Two countries where this phenomenon can be seen working clearly are Canada and Belgium. Canada is important because it is the country where U.S. investment is the greatest, and it therefore provides a clue to what happens as U.S. investment grows large. Americans have invested more than $25 billion in Canada, and they control nearly two-thirds of Canada's mining, manufacturing, and petroleum production. (*New York Times*, Feb. 11, 1968.) This control over so much industry enables the U.S. State Department to influence certain aspects of Canadian foreign policy. For example, it is Canadian policy to trade with China and Cuba. The United States wants to stop this. It therefore asks American corporations to instruct their Canadian subsidiaries not to accept orders destined for those countries. This has been done with cars and trucks, and such indirect subversion of Canadian foreign policy is regarded by many Canadians, as an erosion of Canadian sovereignty.[3]

A similar situation occurred in Belgium in early 1968. A Belgian concern, the Clayson Company of Zedelgem, wanted to sell $1.2 million worth of farm equipment to Cuba. However, in 1963 the American Sperry Rand Corporation had acquired 65 per cent of the Clayson stock and had named three men to the five-man board of directors. Under certain U.S. laws, this control makes the company an American company subject to American regulations, one of which is the requirement of a Treasury Department license to sell to Cuba. The Treasury Department refused the license and so the company could not make the sale. This created bad feeling among Belgian workers because the sale would have meant greater employment.[4]

It can be seen from these examples that American expansionism tends to be a partnership between the U.S. government and American business, each helping the other to exert greater influence and grow more powerful.

The Congress constantly pressures the executive branch to do more to aid business. In April 1968 the House Subcommittee on Foreign Economic Policy published a report on the involvement of U.S. private enterprise in developing countries.

"Present Government programs designed to promote private investment in the less-developed countries are not doing the job," said the report. "This is made apparent by the fact that the present flow of U.S. private investment is on a plateau and has been stagnant for some years. In the opinion of the subcommittee, it would be in the national interest to increase this flow. To achieve this end, it is necessary that existing programs be made more effective and that new and more imaginative programs be adopted. . . . The level of direct governmental aid must be kept sufficient to build an adequate infrastructure, meaning by 'infrastructure' an economic environment that is conducive to private investment, including education, sanitation, transportation, communication, and various governmental institutions." [5]

The Subcommittee recommended a full spectrum of subsidies to increase private investment in the developing nations. The idea is that the taxpayers minimize the risks while the stockholders reap the profits.

The State Department generally responds to Congressional criticism by showing that it is already doing a great deal to help U.S. business overseas. In recent years it has made a particular effort to increase the amount of business investment in the developing areas. In 1967 Anthony M. Solomon, Assistant Secretary of State for Economic Affairs, told a House committee:

"Throughout its history, the State Department has been concerned with private overseas investment. The American private investor has always looked to the Department to protect his legitimate interests overseas and to negotiate the treaties that establish the basic legal framework for his activities abroad. . . . Whether the private investor went abroad or whether he stayed at home was not of great moment to anyone but himself. . . . No government agency urged him to do so. . . .

"Today, this has changed. Our interest in private foreign investment goes well beyond our earlier limited concern. For balance of payments reasons we are asking American investors to limit their capital outflow to the advanced countries. At the same time, we are urging them to increase their investments in the low-income countries. We have the liveliest interest in stimulating U.S. private participation in the economic growth of the developing countries of Asia, Africa, and Latin America." [6]

By 1969 it was evident that this policy of stimulating investment in the developing areas was having some success. In March the Department of Commerce reported a gradual shift of investments away from Canada and Western Europe toward Latin America and other poorer areas. Most of the new investments were in extractive industries with petroleum companies expecting to increase their outlays by 11 percent in 1969. Mining and smelting companies were planning an increase of 13 percent. While total overseas private investment was up about 3 percent, over the previous year, this represented a general decline in the rate of increase which averaged 20 percent a year from 1960 to 1966. [7] Some analysts blamed the declining growth rate on government balance of payments policies.

In answer to criticism of this genre, President Nixon announced in April 1969, a substantial easing of restrictions on the flow of U.S. capital abroad. He signed an executive order reducing taxes on American purchases of foreign securities, and the Federal Reserve Bank at the same time made credit easier for Americans wishing to invest abroad. It was a sign that the Nixon administration would be characterized by accelerated economic expansionism abroad.

The most important statesman to oppose U.S. economic expansion was President Charles DeGaulle of France, and the reasons for this are fairly obvious. In a comprehensive cover story on March 8, 1965, entitled "High Stakes—U.S. Investment in Europe," *Newsweek* magazine reported that "American companies have opened 500 new operations [in France] in the past two years. French national pride is lacerated by the fact that U.S. firms now control almost the whole electronics industry, 90 per cent of the production of synthetic rubber, 65 per cent of petroleum distribution, 65 per cent of farm machinery production. Even a few of the subcontractors for President DeGaulle's top-secret *force de frappe* are U.S. subsidiaries."

The picture for Europe as a whole is even more startling. *Time* magazine reported December 29, 1967: "Americans now control 80% of Europe's computer business, 90% of the microcircuit industry, 40% of its automaking, and sizable shares of chemicals, farm machinery and oil. In Britain, U.S. companies own half of all modern industry, employ one of every 17 British workingmen, manufacture 10% of all British goods for home consumption or export. U.S. firms also squeeze out twice as much profit from invested capital as their British competitors. Of this, they ship $225 million a year home, reinvest the rest for the long term abroad."

It is not difficult to imagine that a continuation of this process at its present rate will soon deprive Europeans of any effective control of their economic affairs, and the loss of economic control is very likely to be followed by the loss of independence in political affairs as well. DeGaulle's resistance to this process was therefore nothing less than an attempt to preserve France as a viable and sovereign nation-state.

There are those, most notably the French publicist Jean-Jacques Servan-Schreiber, who argue that the best way to cope with the phenomenon of American expansionism is to build a strong, federated Western Europe based on a dynamic economy copied from the American model. He does not advocate throwing the Americans out, but rather emulating them and forming commercial alliances with them.[8]

The Servan-Schreiber view is not incompatible with views expressed by powerful American businessmen and statesmen. A good example is George W. Ball, former U.S. Ambassador to the United Nations. Ball sees the business community as providing the leadership in creating a new world system of power configurations. In an article in *Life* magazine, March 28, 1968, he called for the creation of a new world system of three and a half superpowers—the United States, the Soviet Union, a unified Western Europe, and Japan. Ball says that U.S. policy should concentrate on building strong relationships between the industrialized nations of the northern hemisphere. This is where the power is, he declares. What about the poor nations in the southern hemisphere? "Shameful as it undoubtedly is," says Ball, "the world has lived at least two-thirds poor and one-third rich for generations. Unjust as it may be, the power of the poor countries is limited. They can create local situations of instability . . . but they do not, given reasonable prudence on our part, have the capacity to precipitate a major world conflict. . . . Our first priority must be to build a modern structure of power in the

industrialized North. To do this, we must not only encourage
the emergence of a new political unity in Europe but also
make Japan a full member of the club of advanced non-
Communist nations as the principal large modern power in
Asia."

A major role in building this modern structure of power in
the industrialized North is assigned by Ball to American
business. "By gearing their policies," says Ball, "to the world
economy—with respect not only to sales but also to the pro-
curement of raw materials, production, investment and financing—the great American world companies provide man with
a fresh and hopeful vision: the possibility of utilizing resources in accordance with a single objective standard of
efficiency. . . . We should take pride in the American businessmen who, with vigor and a spirit of adventure, are investing their capital in foreign lands. . . . United States
industry is doing exactly what European industry should be
doing: aware of the potential of the world economy, it is
exporting capital for productive investment. How good it
would be for them and for us if European businessmen were
investing vast sums in American mines and farms and factories, mixing the national eggs in a healthful international
omelet."

Ball, a master chef, continued out of government as well as
in to make his contribution to the international omelet. In
March, 1969, he joined the Board of Directors and became
an administrator of Italamerica SA, a new $50-million invest-
ment fund. The fund was announced in a Paris press conference given by Ball and Charles E. Bohlen, former U.S.
Ambassador to France. Bohlen is the President of the fund.
In the United States the roles of diplomat and financier are
frequently interchangeable.

George Ball is clearly proposing a new world system in
which the rich nations combine to preserve their security and

enhance their wealth. He believes that the poor nations will probably be too weak to cause serious trouble. But this particular aspect of the problem is viewed differently by others, as the following news story by Stuart H. Loory, of the *Times-Post Service* illustrates:

"WASHINGTON, May 3, 1967. The Johnson Administration is quietly promoting a speech setting forth the idea that the United States is indeed—and should be—the world's policeman. The speech defends the American involvement in Vietnam as 'the duty of the United States as the richest and most powerful country in the world to enforce the law against aggressive war.' . . .

"The speech was delivered last Friday night at Valparaiso University in Indiana by Thurman Arnold, the senior partner in the Washington law firm of Arnold and Porter, which has close ties with the Administration. A former partner in the firm is Justice Abe Fortas. . . . Mr. Johnson himself, and some aides, have given copies of the speech to visitors in recent days.

"Arnold argued that the majority of American citizens of both political parties believe in the United States' burden, saying:

" 'I think they have learned the lesson that it is the function of a dominant world power, rather than the disorderly consensus of bickering lesser powers like the United Nations, to take the lead in establishing world order and enforcing international law. . . .

" 'Is it arrogance for the United States to enforce international law not for our own selfish interests but in the interest of world peace?

" 'We are the only nation in the world capable of that task.' " [9]

There are subtle but important differences between the Ball view on the one hand, and the Arnold view on the other. Ball emphasizes the constructive role of a dynamic business community in building regional alliances and federations in the northern hemisphere. He proposes what amounts to an alliance of the rich. The police function in the developing world does not worry him much if the rich industrial powers cooperate. Ball minimizes national divisions and wants to strengthen those forces which build relationships among the rich that transcend national boundaries.

The other view is more nationalistic and places greater emphasis on United States initiatives. One of its most important advocates, Irving Kristol, editor of Basic Books, Inc., is a leading protagonist of a Pax Americana. "The world," writes Kristol, "*does* rely on American power, does count on American power, does look to American power for the preservation of a decent level of international law and order." [10] The central focus of the world system according to Kristol is an imperial America. "The United States is not going to cease being an imperial power," he wrote in the July 1967 *Foreign Affairs*, "no matter what happens in Viet Nam or elsewhere. It is the world situation—and the history which created this situation—that appoints imperial powers. . . ."

Ball on the one hand is an internationalist. He wants to integrate the rich, industrial nations and unify them politically. Kristol, on the other hand, is essentially a nationalist. He wants the United States to police the world. The issue is multilateral versus unilateral expansionism. While there are these differences, the similarities of the two approaches are more important. Both are more concerned with power than with values, and they are both expansionist. Both are designed primarily to protect the rich and ignore or restrain the poor.

The Peace Corps as it presently functions, is compatible with either view, for it strengthens the position of the United States in the developing world. The following chapters will explain how it performs this role.

III: MACAULAYISM

"We have no need to apologize for our position in India or to adopt the attitude of humanitarian cranks, usually profoundly ignorant of the facts of history, who regard our Indian Empire as a crime, and, while concentrating on the more questionable dealings of a less scrupulous age, ignore the rescue of hundreds of millions of their fellow-men from chaotic misery and the peace and prosperity that we have established. Our Indian Empire was developed, not as the result of a deliberate policy of greed and grab, but by the force of circumstances, first in defense of our trade Settlements, later by the pressure of European competitors—Portuguese, Dutch and French—and finally by the need for tranquility in the Provinces that had come under our care. And if the price of Empire must be paid in blood and service, 'Lord God, we ha' paid in full!' So far from having anything to be ashamed of, we have every reason for pride in our Indian Empire and in the work that we have accomplished. On the other hand, there is no justification for an attitude of swaggering superiority. India is not, and never was, a conquered country. We owe our position there to our attitude of impartiality towards conflicting races and religions, and to certain qualities of character, which offered to torn and distracted communities the prospect of peace and freedom and of justice between man and man. Questions as to racial equality seem to me to be beside the point. What race is there that should claim superiority to people that gave to the world a Buddha, an Asoka and an Akbar, religions and philosophies that embrace every religion and school of thought that has ever existed, an epic literature perhaps unrivaled, and some of the greatest masterpieces in the realm of human art? But there is a difference between Indians and ourselves, and that is why the Empire grew up and why we are still in India."

Evan Maconochie, "Life in the Indian C i v i l Service" (1926), pp. 249-250.

In the days when empires were respectable, one of the greatest was the British, and it became a cliché to remark, as scores of writers did, that the brightest jewel in the imperial crown was India. The quality of that brightness depended upon your point of view. For an Englishman it might have

been the brillance of economic development represented by
the vast irrigation system built by the British in the Punjab.
For an Indian it might have been the shocking glare of
General Dyer's massacre of peaceful demonstrators in
Amritsar.

But however one judged its moral qualities, the control for
more than 200 years by a relative handful of Englishmen
over the destinies of hundreds of millions of Indians was a
remarkable achievement. It was also an achievement that
made Englishmen very rich, so many in fact, that a Bengali
word, *nabob*, was brought into the English language to
describe them.

The British conquest of India began with business, not
with armies. It started with the East India Company, a private company which was given a charter by the Crown in
1600 to engage in trade in India. These Englishmen of John
Company, as it was called, were not conquerors, but traders.
They found India disunited, and without strong government.
To protect themselves and their warehouses, the men of John
Company recruited their own private armies. The weakness
of the feuding Indians enhanced the power of the Company
and gradually it began to take over the task of preserving
law and order. Then to pay for this governmental service it
began levying taxes. Before long the Company was administering justice and functioning as sovereign in the entire subcontinent. By 1757 it was doing more governing than trading,
and by 1833 it was no longer a business at all, but a government pure and simple.[1]

There is more to the history of British imperialism in India
than John Company's transition from business to government,
and the fact that so few Englishmen were able to maintain
control over so many Indians and so vast a territory for so
long a time requires more explanation than to point out the
disunity of Indians and the military superiority of the British.

The British did not control India with only her crack regiments or even with the loyal Ghurkas and Sikhs, but with an adroit combination of force and good works. The British began the process of modernization in India, and there were enough Indians who wanted to be modernized to give the British a supportive constituency. These Indians formed a new elite which helped to Anglicize the subcontinent, and protect it from revolutionary currents like those that eventually brought Mao Tse-tung to power in China.

The early days of East India Company rule in India were characterized by enormous corruption. Appointments to the civil service were by patronage and were given to boys as young as 15. In India they enjoyed tremendous power and authority over the local population, and they rarely exercised it with wisdom and humility. It was only the lazy and the unimaginative among them that could not make a personal fortune in the conduct of private trade, which was one of the perquisites of appointment to the Indian Civil Service (ics).

Eventually there were reforms. Private trade was banned and appointment to the Civil Service was by competitive examination. Successful applicants were dubbed "competition wallahs" to distinguish them from the older patronage appointees, and they were given extensive training at a special school, Haileybury College, before they were sent out to India.

Gradually the Civil Service became a highly qualified, effective governing force in whose ranks there were many who sincerely desired not to exploit India, but to give the Indians good government. It was such men who helped the Indians build the foundation of public works, parliamentary institutions, education, and commitment to modernization upon which independent India and Pakistan have based their attempts to construct democracy and prosperity in the subcontinent.

If India was to be modernized, two things were vital: an
efficient legal system and western education. Both were necessary to give legitimacy to the modernizing process, and
each was dependent on the other. Western education was
needed to introduce science and technology and to sweep
away the encrustations of superstition which smothered development and change. Law was required to blend Hindu,
Muslim, and other cultures into a single political community
where order could be maintained. Law and education, then,
were the cement which fastened India more securely to
Britain. While the bond was strong, the force of arms was
unnecessary. Without it, all the soldiers of the crown could
never have pacified India.

One of the men who understood this best was an intellectual
of Scottish ancestry, Thomas Babington Macaulay (1800-
1859). Macaulay's greatest claim to fame is as a historian
and essayist, but he is also important as an example of the
intellectual in politics. He was elected to parliament and
served in two cabinets, in one as Secretary of State for War.

Macaulay's political philosophy was similar to that of
twentieth century American liberals. He was a humanitarian
reformer who believed in working within the existing system
to achieve change. Although he was a part of what today
would be called the Establishment, he never gave up his independence of mind. For example, while he was a member of
the Cabinet, a bill to free the slaves of the West Indies came
before the House of Commons. What might have been a good
bill was badly compromised by a clause which would have
required freed slaves to work as "apprentices" to their former owners for an undetermined period. Clearly this was a
prolongation of slavery under another name. Because of this
clause, Macaulay could not approve the bill. But to oppose
it would put him in opposition to the government of which he
was a member. His insecure financial position and the pend-

ing possibility of a more lucrative position meant that
Macaulay would risk a great deal if he refused to go along
with the government. Nevertheless, he determined to do so.
Not only did he vote against the measure, but he spoke out
against it in the House. He also submitted his resignation
from the government, which the cabinet wisely decided not
to accept. Largely due to his efforts, the West Indies bill was
greatly improved, and before long slavery was abolished in
all the British colonies.

The more lucrative position about which Macaulay was
concerned when his principles forced him to oppose the government was an appointment to the Supreme Council of the
East India Company. This was a job that paid ten thousand
pounds a year. Macaulay was confident he could live in India
on five thousand and save the rest. Thus he could return to
England after three years (at the age of forty) and have "with
the accruing interest" a sum of thirty thousand pounds. This
would not make him rich but would give him what he called
a "competence", enough to eliminate the major risks of political independence.

Macaulay received the appointment and went out to India
in 1834 where he was also appointed President of the Law
Commission charged with designing a new penal code. He
remained in India until 1838. In slightly less than four years
he made an impact on the subcontinent every bit as important as the marks left by Clive and Warren Hastings.

Macaulay was a pragmatist who distrusted theory. "I rest
my opinion on no general theory of government," he said. "I
distrust all general theories of government." Nevertheless
Macaulay's political philosophy owed a great deal to theor-
ists such as James Mill and Jeremy Bentham, and like them,
he was part of the Whig-Utilitarian-Liberal tradition which
was committed to such ideas as the rule of law, civil liberty,

freedom of the press, representative government, and an independent judiciary.

India presented a problem for the men who believed in
these ideals, because the government of India under the East
India Company was a despotism which provided none of
these benefits. How could a liberal believe in freedom for
Englishmen but accede to a despotic government for Indians?
On the other hand, since India had been despotic before the
British came, what right would Englishmen have to impose
democratic institutions? Perhaps it would be better to withdraw and simply leave the Indians to their own devices.

The liberals had answers to these questions. While it may
have been a mistake to go into India in the first place, they
said, Britain was now there and it would be irresponsible
simply to withdraw. One could not abandon those Indians
who had come to depend upon Britain for security and order.
For Britain to leave India would merely be to condemn the
country to the depredations of hundreds of warring tyrants.
It would also leave a power vacuum that might encourage
expansionism by Tsarist Russia.

However, the liberals said, the Indians were not sufficiently mature politically for representative government and
democratic institutions. "Utterly out of the question," said
James Mill. "We know India cannot have a free government," said Macaulay. "But she may have the next best
thing—a firm and impartial despotism." [2] Therefore, the liberals argued, it should be the aim of the British *Raj* to provide the *benefits* of self-government without the *mechanism* of
self-government. "We have to engraft on despotism," said
Macaulay, "those blessings which are the natural fruits of
liberty." [3]

Macaulay argued that an area in which despotism had
inherent advantages was that of jurisprudence, where India
had serious problems. "I believe," said Macaulay, "that no

country ever stood so much in need of a code of laws as
India. . . . We have now in our Eastern empire Hindu law,
Mohammedan law, Parsee law, English law, perpetually
mingling with each other, and disturbing each other; varying with the person, varying with the place. . . . The only
Mohammedan book in the nature of a code is the Koran;—
the only Hindu book the Institutes. Everybody who knows
those books, knows that they provide for a very small part of
the cases which must arise in every community." [4]

A despotism, Macaulay argued, could make order out of
this chaos far better than could a democracy. "A code," he
told the British parliament, "is almost the only blessing—
perhaps it is the only blessing which absolute governments
are better fitted to confer on a nation than popular governments. The work of digesting a vast and artificial system of
unwritten jurisprudence, is far more easily performed, and
far better performed by few minds than by many . . . A
quiet knot of two or three veteran jurists is an infinitely better
machinery for such a purpose than a large popular assembly
divided, as such assemblies almost always are, into adverse
factions. This seems to me, therefore, to be precisely that
point of time at which the advantages of a complete written
code of laws may most easily be conferred on India. It is a
work which cannot be well performed in an age of barbarism—which cannot without great difficulty be performed
in an age of freedom. It is the work which especially belongs
to a government like that of India—to an enlightened and
paternal despotism." [5]

But while Macaulay was willing to impose a code of laws
on the Indians, he was not willing to say that they should
always be governed by Englishmen. Macaulay's position was
that the benevolent paternalism of British rule should prepare the Indians for eventual self-government, and that it
would be "the proudest day in English history" when the

Indians could take over the institutions established by the foreigners and run them themselves. That day occurred on August 15, 1947. But did it mean the end of empire?

For Macaulay the real empire was not the empire of viceroys and British civil servants, but something more subtle. "There is an empire," he told parliament, "exempt from all natural causes of decay . . . That empire is the imperishable empire of our arts and our morals, our literature and our laws."[6] The key to establishing that empire was in education, particularly the education of an elite.

"It is impossible for us," wrote Macaulay in his famous 1835 Minute on Education, "with our limited means, to attempt to educate the body of the people. We must at present do our best to form a class who may be interpreters between us and the millions whom we govern; a class of persons, Indian in blood and color, but English in taste, in opinions, in morals, and in intellect."[7]

This class of Indians, Indian in blood but English in taste, opinions, morals, and intellect would preserve the good will toward England that would be necessary to retain the commercial advantages that Englishmen had won. "It is scarcely possible," Macaulay told parliament, "to calculate the benefits which we might derive from the diffusion of European civilization among the vast population of the East. It would be, on the most selfish view of the case, far better for us that the people of India were well-governed and independent of us, than ill-governed and subject to us; that they were ruled by their own kings, but wearing our broadcloth, and working with our cutlery, than they were performing their salaams to English collectors and English magistrates, but were too ignorant to value, or too poor to buy, English manufactures. To trade with civilized men is infinitely more profitable than to govern savages."[8]

A more complete statement of this point of view was made

by Macaulay's brother-in-law, Charles Trevelyan, in a pamphlet entitled *The Education of the People of India* published in 1838.

"The existing connections between two such distant countries as England and India, cannot, in the nature of things, be permanent: no effort or policy can prevent the natives from ultimately regaining their independence. But there are two ways of arriving at this point. One of these is through the medium of revolution; the other, through that of reform. In one, the forward movement is sudden and violent; in the other, it is gradual and peaceable. One must end in the complete alienation of mind and separation of interests between ourselves and the natives; the other in a permanent alliance, founded on mutual benefit and good-will. The only means at our disposal for preventing the one and securing the other class of results is, to set the natives on a process of European improvement, to which they are already sufficiently inclined. They will then cease to desire and aim at independence on the old Indian footing . . . The political education of a nation is a work of time; and while it is in progress, we shall be as safe as it will be possible for us to be. The natives will not rise against us, we shall stoop to raise them; there will be no reaction, because there will be no pressure; the national activity will be fully and harmlessly employed in acquiring and diffusing European knowledge, and in naturalising European institutions. The educated classes, knowing that the elevation of their country on these principles can only be worked out under our protection, will naturally cling to us . . . The change will thus be peaceably and gradually effected; there will be no struggle, no mutual exasperation; the natives will have independence, after first learning how to make good use of it; and we shall exchange profitable subjects for still more profitable allies. The present administrative connection benefits families, but a strict com-

mercial union between the first manufacturing and the first
producing country in the world, would be a solid foundation
of strength and prosperity to our whole nation. If this course
be adopted, there will, properly speaking, be no separation.
A precarious and temporary relation will almost imper-
ceptibly pass into another far more durable and beneficial.
Trained by us to happiness and independence, and endowed
with our learning and political institutions, India will remain
the proudest monument of British benevolence; and we shall
long continue to reap, in the affectionate attachment of the
people, and in a great commercial intercourse with their
splendid country, the fruit of that liberal and enlightened
policy which suggested to us this line of conduct." [9]

From the writings of Macaulay and other British liberals
it is possible to distill certain principles regarding the best
relationship between Britain, an advanced industrial state
and India, a technologically backward country.

1. Because of its values and its technology, English culture
is superior to the cultures of India, and its dissemination is a
service to the recipients as well as to Britain. "A single shelf
of a good European library," wrote Macaulay, "was worth
the whole native literature of India and Arabia."

2. The English language is the best vehicle for the dissemination of English culture.

3. The aim of Britain should be the creation of an English
speaking elite, tied to the mother country by taste, opinion,
morals and intellect. This elite will help preserve a hospita-
ble climate for British commercial interests, and will sym-
pathetically interpret other British actions to the Indian
masses.

4. The survival and growth of British culture and influence, and commercial opportunity in India depend more on
good works and education than they do on military force.

It is obvious that these principles reflect considerable

cultural arrogance, although in fairness to Macaulay it must
be pointed out that he did not want to destroy indigenous
culture. His draft of the penal code attempted to preserve
as much Hindu and Muslim law as could be fairly administered. "We propose no rash innovation," he said. "We
wish to give no shock to the prejudices of any part of our
subjects. Our principle is simply this—uniformity where
you can have it—diversity where you must have it—but in
all cases certainty."

Macaulay pointed out that Hindu law had been superseded
by Mohammedan law in many parts of India long before the
arrival of the British, and it, in turn had already been superseded by English law where John Company had ruled. The
problem was simply to bring order and fairness out of chaos.

Yet order is a cultural value which some peoples may
regard more as an imposition than a blessing. To promote
it in cultures where it is not appreciated, may in fact be in
the best interests of the people of those cultures, as I believe
it was in the case of India. But those are my values speaking, not necessarily the Indians', and the degree of arrogance
involved in a nation's advancing them is measured by the
vigor and effectiveness of the means.

However, a state cannot divest itself of its culture, and if
it is active in international affairs, it will inevitably promote
its cultural values one way or another. One cannot fault
Macaulay, who did not send the East India Company into
India in the first place, for wanting to give the Indians the
best that Britain had to offer them.

While the Macaulay approach was never pursued with
sufficient zeal to make it a complete success, it did have a
remarkable impact. It did create a Westernized elite which
eventually took over the governance of the two new nations
of India and Pakistan, and despite fluctuations in foreign
policy, India today continues to be close to Britain, and even

closer to her senior Anglo-Saxon partner, the United States. While regional particularism prevents the effective use of any indigenous language as a national medium of communication, English remains the essential tool of government, science, education, justice, politics, and the press. The members of the Indian ruling elite today are more English in tastes, morals, and intellect than they are able to conceal with their *Khadi* clothing.

While Macaulayism made British rule in India more benevolent, it also prolonged it by making it seem less objectionable. It gave British sovereignty a legitimacy, and hence a stability, which the force of arms alone could never have provided. I have described these ideas of Macaulay and the British liberals at length because I believe that they originated, articulated, and practiced a philosophy which, in an updated form, is implicit in the overseas role of the Peace Corps. This philosophy can be seen in action most clearly in the United States trust of Micronesia where the Peace Corps is helping to develop a legal system and teaching English to the local inhabitants. But it also operates in the countries which are semi-colonial such as Liberia, Thailand, and Panama, and in others where American business is expanding but where American political influence is still minimal.

The urge to expand, to be world leaders, to set the style of life for people everywhere is a powerful one that extends beyond those who merely see the prospects for personal gain. It is found even more strongly among the liberals than among the conservatives. A good example is Warren Wiggins, Deputy Director of the Peace Corps under Shriver, and a man of dedication, humanity and vision. "America must go abroad," he told the California Teachers Association in 1963. "It is our only hope. If we in America—through organization such as yours—don't go abroad, we will find our once rich, easy, healthy, and educated society distorted, disfigured, and ultimately overwhelmed by world forces. We will either lead or be led."[10]

The twentieth century world is not the same as that of the nineteenth, even though certain modes of influence persist. In the nineteenth, Macaulayism mitigated the unfairness and elevated the content of an already established political control. The pattern in India began with business, which was followed by conquest, and then came Macaulayism. Today, Macaulayism, manifested in the Peace Corps, may precede the other two. It may be, in Sargent Shriver's phrase, the "point of the lance." In any case, its major function is to assist in the expansion of American cultural values to develop pro-American, English-speaking elites, and to make America's role in world affairs, whatever it may be, more palatable.

IV: THE PURPOSE OF THE CORPS

> "There are, of course, a good many hundreds of millions of people scattered throughout the world and you will come in contact with only a few, but the great impression of what kind of country we have and what kind of people we are will depend on their judgment in these countries of you.
>
> "You will be the personification of a special group of young Americans, and if you can impress them with your commitment to freedom, to the advancement of the interests of people everywhere, to your pride in your country and in its best traditions and what it stands for, the influence may be far-reaching and will go far beyond the immediate day to day tasks that you may do in the months that are ahead."
>
> *President John F. Kennedy in remarks to the first group of Volunteers to be sent overseas. August 28, 1961.*

The name "Peace Corps" is good for public relations but poor as description of the organization's activities and mission. It does not make peace between warring nations; neither does it play a conciliating role between nations that are on the brink of war. If its name were to be taken seriously, then one would have to assume that the only nations likely to go to war are the poor nations, for it is there that the Peace Corps is sent. It does not go to the USSR, to Germany, to France, or to China to make those peoples less likely to engage in war. Neither does it go to make peace between Israel and Egypt.

The Peace Corps, of course, is aware of all this, but insists that it is promoting peace nevertheless. "What is its contribution to peace?" asked Associate Director Harris Wofford. "The basic proposition, of course, is that peace is not merely the absence of war but the presence of justice, and that twentieth-century justice requires universal education and development. As carriers of twentieth-century technology and agents of peaceful change, Volunteers are, thus, indeed contributing to peace." [1]

This approach raises several questions. Does the introduction of new technology contribute to justice, or to the creation of economically privileged technical elites? Does the peaceful change encouraged by the Peace Corps lead to significant advances toward justice, or does it merely deflate revolutionary pressures in those areas where violent overthrow of the existing order may, in fact, be the only pragmatic alternative? In other words, is the peace-making contribution of the Peace Corps essentially its capacity to prevent a particular kind of war, namely, revolutionary war?

Whatever the answers to these questions, and subsequent chapters of this book will suggest some, there does not seem to be any evidence that any carefully thought-out theory of change played much of a role in the conception and early design of the Peace Corps. Indeed, it appears to have come into existence as much by accident as by design when John F. Kennedy seized upon the idea as a gimmick in the presidential election campaign of 1960.

Kennedy profited greatly from a latent Macaulayism present in America that year. It was due, more than anything else, to the enormous popular and official interest in the book by William J. Lederer and Eugene Burdick, *The Ugly American*. A Book-of-the-Month Club selection in October 1958, this fictionalized critique of American representatives abroad went through twenty printings the first year, and was eventually made into an extravagant, if rather dreary, motion picture. While the book contained many inaccuracies, and was grossly unfair in important respects, it did succeed in focusing public attention on some of the more glaring defects of the American effort in the developing countries. It also made the public acutely aware of the need for better foreign language training in elementary and secondary schools.[2]

The Ugly American was a major factor in preparing public opinion for the creation of the Peace Corps. It did this, no doubt, by persuading many Americans that the United States was losing the battle for men's minds in Asia, because American representatives there had little contact with, or understanding of, the rural areas, because they didn't speak the local languages, and because they lived luxuriously in the big cities, more concerned with the niceties of protocol in the social clubs than with the real needs of ordinary people. "The Russians will win the world," said one of the fictional heroes of the book, "by their successes in a multitude of tiny battles . . . in the rice fields of Asia, at village meetings, in schools; but mainly they will take place in the minds of men." [3]

In what they called a "factual epilogue" appended to the book, Lederer and Burdick pointed out that American representation could be better: "In extensive interviews with superior graduating seniors, the authors have discovered that the brightest seniors reject foreign service because it is 'too dull, too bureaucratic.' Many of these students would be attracted to overseas duty if the standards were higher, if contact with natives were possible, if the 'good living' were not stressed so much and the challenge stressed more."

The speech in which presidential candidate John F. Kennedy spelled out the Peace Corps idea was made at the San Francisco Cow Palace November 2, 1960. It reads almost as if it has been cribbed from *The Ugly American.*

"Teachers, doctors, technicians and experts desperately needed in a dozen fields by under-developed nations—are pouring forth from Moscow to advance the cause of world communism. . . .

"They know the country, they speak the language—and in Guinea, Ghana, Laos and all over the globe, they are working fast and effectively. . . .

"They can only be countered by Americans equally skilled and equally dedicated—and if I am elected I ask you to help me find those Americans. . . ."

Then, on this anti-Communist foundation, Kennedy built a more Macaulay-like structure:

"Where are we going to obtain the technicians needed to work with the people of under-developed lands outside the normal diplomatic channels—and by technicians I include engineers, doctors, teachers, agricultural experts, specialists in public law, labor taxation, civil service—all the skills necessary to establish a viable economy, a stable government and a decent standard of living. . . .

"Think of the wonders skilled American personnel could work, building goodwill, building the peace. . . .

"I therefore propose that our inadequate efforts in this area be supplemented by a 'peace corps' of talented young men willing and able to serve their country in this fashion for three years as an alternative to peacetime Selective Service—well qualified through rigorous standards—well trained in the language, skills and customs they will need to know. . . .

"This would be a volunteer corps—and volunteers would be sought among talented young women as well—and from every race and walk of life. For this nation is full of young people eager to serve the cause of peace in the most useful way. . . ."

Then, in conclusion, Kennedy went back to anti-Communism: "I am convinced that our young men and women, dedicated to freedom, are fully capable of overcoming the efforts of Mr. Khrushchev's missionaries who are dedicated to undermining that freedom." [4]

As the Kennedy speech makes clear, the Peace Corps was originally conceived as an instrument with which to fight Communism, although it was also meant to be more than that. According to the act of Congress which established it,

the Corps has three purposes. The first is to help developing
countries meet their needs for trained manpower. The second
is to promote a better understanding of other peoples by
Americans, and the third is to help other peoples understand
Americans. According to the Peace Corps, these are essentially non-political goals, and the Corps is not an instrument
of American foreign policy. "A volunteer is on his own, and
we won't have it any other way," Director Jack Vaughn said
at UCLA in 1966. "He is not an instrument of American foreign policy." [5] And two years later Vaughn told the Senate
Foreign Relations Committee: "It was established in the
early days of the Peace Corps that this movement would not
be a part of U.S. foreign policy. This position has been
reiterated and I think faithfully followed. So, instead, the
Peace Corps is a movement of our society." [6]

This is nonsense. The Peace Corps is no more a movement
than is the United States Information Agency or the CIA,
but it is just as much an instrument of U.S. foreign policy
as they are. All of its overseas programs are planned in careful consultation with Embassy and AID representatives (the
U.S. Ambassador in each country must approve all projects),
and there is an elaborate multi-agency review procedure in
Washington with vetoes all along the line. Moreover, it was
sold to Congress primarily as a propaganda device with which
to fight Communism and improve America's image abroad.
Hubert Humphrey made this clear when he carried the Peace
Corps bill on the floor of the Senate and read into the Record
a document prepared for him by the Peace Corps. "There is
no better way to counteract anti-American propaganda," it
said, "than by providing contact between Americans and
citizens of other countries. . . . The bright, young, dedicated
Americans who will constitute the Peace Corps are the finest
fruits of our way of life and the best ambassadors this country can produce. Simply by living and working abroad . . .

they can do more to serve the image of this country abroad
than all the counter-propaganda that money can buy." [7]

George Ball, when he was Under Secretary of State, spoke
frankly about the Peace Corps as an instrument of foreign
policy when he appeared before the House Foreign Affairs
Committee in 1962. The following exchange took place—

Rep. Monagan: ". . . Mr. Secretary, I suppose that in
appraising the usefulness of the Peace Corps as an instrument of our policy we have to balance the utility against the
amount of money we are spending for it.

"You would agree with that?"

Mr. Ball: "I would agree with that."

Rep. Monagan: " . . . What I would like to ask . . . is just
exactly where is it that the impact of this program is most
important. In what field is it that we get the greatest benefit? . . ."

Mr. Ball: "Obviously this is one, merely one, element in
activities which must be very big and varied if American
policy is to succeed around the world.

"There are, I would think, several ways in which the Peace
Corps contributes to the advancement of American policy.

"First, and I would think perhaps at the top of the list,
I would put the fact of its existence and *what it symbolizes*
in terms of the interests of young Americans in creating the
kind of friendships that these Americans are developing in
the work they are doing.

"Secondly, the kind of tangible assistance that can be
given, particularly in *education in the teaching of English* to
students that otherwise wouldn't have the benefit of it.

"But even more again than the teaching of English, there
is the association of these young teachers with the students
with whom they are working, the kind of *relationships that
can be established that way.*

"To the world this means *giving a kind of quality and char-*

acter of generosity to the American effort. To some extent, therefore, it tends *to combat the attacks on America,* wholly unjustified of course, but in some places marginally effective, that our AID effort is a form of commercial or economic penetration.

"Certainly the young Peace Corps volunteers could never be accused of anything of that sort. The very fact that they are prepared to live under conditions that are similar to the conditions and environment of the local people, is an evidence of the fact that Americans are not simply concerned with the creature comforts and the enjoyment of the highest standard of living in the world. . . .

"I think in some countries it might have some real effect in *changing the character of the attitude toward the United States.* In other countries it might not be so effective. . . .

"I would suppose that we probably are getting more for our money in the Peace Corps than in almost anything we are doing. . . ."

Rep. Monagan: "It is in terms of the image, the propaganda effect upon the people of the country with whom these Peace Corps volunteers come in contact, is that your feeling?"

Mr. Ball: "Yes, and the publicity they get, the *image that they create,* all these intangible." (Emphasis added.)[8]

The first Peace Corps Director, Sargent Shriver, stressed the soft-sell propaganda role of the Corps in his first appearance before the House Appropriations Committee in 1961:

"We do not expect our Peace Corps volunteers to have very much influence, directly, on Prime Ministers and Cabinet members and political leaders. We don't expect Peace Corps volunteers to be aggressive in arguing immediate political causes. We do expect—and *our selection and training processes are so designed*—that our Peace Corps volunteers can, with pride and conviction, talk about the United States of America, and we expect that their living and working arrangements, attitudes, and general demeanor will help to balance out some of the unfortunate impressions that people in other countries have developed about some Americans overseas." (Emphasis added.)[9]

The following year Shriver pointed out that for the Corps to be effective it was necessary that it not look like a propaganda agency. "We have been chary," he told the Senate Appropriations Committee, ". . . of identifying our operation too closely with the USIA operation abroad, at least at the beginning, because we didn't want the host country to feel that the Peace Corps was coming there as a part of the propaganda effort of the U.S. Government." He went on to explain how he had rejected an offer by USIA to make a film on the Peace Corps and show it in the host country before the arrival of volunteers. Shriver said his approach was to get the host government to do the publicizing. It is a good technique to avoid the stigma of foreign propaganda.

There is evidence that the Peace Corps is one of the most effective, although not necessarily the most economical, propaganda agencies of any government. In 1966 it was asked by the House Appropriations Committee to estimate the number of host country nationals directly served by volunteers up to that time. The Corps responded with a chart which showed that over a five year period 20,000 volunteers had directly served 4,300,000 citizens of the host countries.[10] Given the fact that the total cost of the Peace Corps to that point had been approximately $400,000,000, the cost per host country national reached was less than $100. This is not as expensive as it appears when one remembers the length, quality, and intensity of exposure. Arnold Zeitlin, a Volunteer in Ghana, thought the cost-effectiveness ratio in Ghana was especially good. "Speaking of cost," he wrote in his book *To the Peace Corps with Love*, "with fifty-one Americans in twenty-seven schools meeting 8000 Ghanian

students every day, the cost-per-thousand-impressions to the
United States would have gladdened the heart of the meanest
media buyer on Madison Avenue." [11]

Another volunteer, Boris Sojka, who served in Somalia
said: "The actual concrete help that we are giving is minis-
cule. The biggest thing, and maybe the best, is acting as
public relations men, showing what Americans are like. This
I think is a complete success." [12]

Frederic C. Thomas, the Peace Corps Director in Morocco
1963-64, described the way that Volunteers accomplished
this public relations task: "He [the PCV] is highly visible,
and he is liked. In a town of five or ten thousand, he is
known to almost everyone. He makes numerous acquaint-
ances and several close friends. The impression he makes
is highly personal, vivid and lasting. The things he says and
does are remembered: that he took a real interest in the
community, that he organized extra-curricular activities, that
he knew what is proper, maybe that he fasted during Rama-
dan, or tried to, and that he took pride in wearing his burnous
rather than merely finding it amusing as a tourist would.
In a society which views itself in highly personal, rather than
institutional, terms, he is the representative American. In
fact, he becomes the stereotype . . ." [13]

The importance of this kind of propaganda work is
attested to by American Ambassadors all over the world.
In Asia, the then Ambassador to India, John Kenneth Galbraith, said in 1961: "The reaction in India has been ex-
ceedingly favorable as a welcome affirmation of American
idealism. It is particularly important in rubbing out the
impression that we are excessively prone to military solutions." [14]

Regarding Africa, the former Ambassador to Nigeria told
of how he gave a Volunteer a lift to his village. "I must
say," he said, "it did my heart good to see the reaction of

the local populace. They were all out there, and if I brought them a million dollars, they couldn't have been as pleased as they were with this one young lad, who was going to teach in this institution." [15]

And from Latin America, the U.S. Ambassador to Colombia, told the House Foreign Affairs Committee: "The affection and respect that is felt for the volunteers by the Colombian villagers is a palpable thing that can be noted even by the most casual observer visiting the villages. Tearful farewells are commonplace when volunteers are transferred . . . Thousands of Colombians [get] a first hand acquaintance with some very unugly Americans [which] goes a long way toward justifying the program and assuring the U.S. taxpayer of a good return on his money." [16]

It is clear that the Peace Corps *is* an instrument of U.S. foreign policy, specifically a propaganda or public relations instrument. Whatever it may be in the minds of the more naive volunteers, this is clearly what it is to the State Department and the Congress.

There is nothing wrong with this in and of itself in my opinion. There is no reason why a great power should not develop new and innovative techniques of conducting international relations, and there is nothing inherently wrong with propagada. Moreover, the development of any instrumentality of foreign policy which is non-military and non-violent, as the Peace Corps is, should be welcome.

However, there are aspects of this particular situation that merit critical examination. First, there is the way the Peace Corps is sold, not to the Congress, but to the volunteers and to world public opinion. Secondly, there is the content of the propaganda message which it transmits to the host country nations with whom it comes in contact. In both of these areas it is deceptive and dishonest. To prospective volunteers it is presented essentially as a vehicle with which to serve humanity, to help build a strong peace. "For as with Peace Corps Volunteers everywhere," Jack Vaughn told the students at UCLA, "their concern has precious little to do with politics and power. They are concerned with serving people—not as guardians of Peace, but by imparting utility and virtue to Peace itself . . . You ask our policy, then? I will say: It is to wage Peace, by dedicating ourselves to the task of lending virtue to Peace for years to come."[17]

This is mawkish rhetoric and it bears little relation to the truth. The policy of the Peace Corps, like the policy of all other instruments of American foreign policy, is to advance the national interest of the United States, or rather what the executive branch of the government conceives to be the national interest. The Corps does this, not by lending virtue to peace, which for those who have known war, needs no such loan, but by lending *the appearance* of virtue to U.S. foreign policy.

The appearance of virtue which the Peace Corps projects for the United States has many facets. One is the notion that Americans are especially altruistic. "The Peace Corps shows what we stand for," said the late Senator Robert F. Kennedy, "not a selfish society but a society that's interested in other people." Another facet of the image is, as Ambassador Galbraith pointed out, the assertion that we are not "excessively prone to military solutions."

But to say this is to mislead, if not to deceive. The American people are certainly no worse than most others, but if one looks at the way they allocate their resources, it is hard to make the case that the United States is very altruistic. Even its international charity must be described as a device to stop Communism if it is to be acceptable to the general public. The size of its foreign aid program is more a function of its gross national product and the phenomenon of expansionism than of superior qualities of altruism, inherent in the American people. And as for its attitude toward military solutions to political problems, mentioned by Ambassador Galbraith, the staggering size of our military-industrial complex, and the willingness to use force in Cuba, the Dominican Republic, Vietnam, and elsewhere, show that the U.S. is at least as prone to resort to violence as any other world power. The facts are that Americans, who do indeed have many virtues, acquired their territory by force and violence, and now behave very selfishly toward Indians, Blacks, Chicanos, and other minorities. And as the failure to pass effective gun control legislation demonstrates, the U.S. has an obsession with the instruments of violence. To obscure or gloss over such facts as the Peace Corps does, is to mislead and to delay the understanding that the people of developing areas need in order to make sound decisions about how much American penetration they want in their countries.

While the Peace Corps practices a double deception, misleading prospective volunteers at home and host country nationals abroad, there are some factors which mitigate the immorality. One is that a certain amount of deception, in the form of exaggeration, is probably inseparable from salesmanship and politics, regardless of the product or the nationality. Peace Corps officials may have to overstate cases in order to survive in Congress, for the perception of subtleties is not among the strong points of most congressmen. Similarly, a certain amount of romantic rhetoric is necessary on the college campuses, if for no other reason than to compete for attention in a semantic environment where modest phraseology has lost ground to the epithet and the obscenity. Moreover, there are many sincere Peace Corps bureaucrats who refuse to believe that the America characterized by racism, decaying cities, and the Vietnam war can be a major part of the true America. They feel that America has some-

thing good to give to the world, and that the world will be
better for it. As their rhetoric becomes more florid these
beliefs approach the status of dogma. But if the rhetoric
does not blind them to the facts, then they agonize over ways
to change the Peace Corps and somehow reconcile the reality
with the dream.

One of the best examples of the kind of soul searching
that goes on within the Peace Corps was an analogy suggested
by a Peace Corps staff member during a recruiting trip to
Berkeley in 1968. "The Peace Corps in the village," he said,
"becomes like the beautiful daughter of the tyrant—the
tyrant parent dealing in the city, dragging out the daughter
to prove he has good genes, selling her body unbeknownst
to her, keeping her dancing and making love in one village
while burning down the next; throwing her a scrap or two
while feeding steak to the village burners." But he argued
that the more beautiful the daughter, the more obvious would
become the brutality of the parent. The beautiful daughter
should not be abandoned, but should be rescued.

The staff man who said these things is no longer with the
Peace Corps.

V: THE VOLUNTEERS

"... the moment a Peace Corps Volunteer begins to feel that he is *not* special, that is the moment he begins to lose his effectiveness. And the moment the Peace Corps loses the mystique of a special calling is the moment we might as well turn it over to any of the other government agencies in Washington that have tried for four years to absorb us. . . .

"You *are* special citizens. You are special citizens because you are *volunteers*, and a volunteer is a person who in a free, democratic society, decided to serve that society—who by a conscious act of his or her free will, has left the ranks of the bystanders and spectators to become a participant. A volunteer is a person with a large ego—and he should be. He is a person with a split personality—wondering on the one hand if he really can make a difference, and knowing on the other hand that he *must* make a difference.

"When you begin to think you are average, my only advice to you is simply: go back to your split-level homes, turn on your television sets, drink your beer—somebody else with a special sense of his individual worth will step up to serve in the Peace Corps."

> *Bill Moyers, then Special Assistant to President Johnson, former Deputy Director of the Peace Corps, March 1965.*

In the American culture the word "volunteer" usually refers to an individual who works for a civic or charitable organization without remuneration—for example, the ladies who ring doorbells for the March of Dimes. But there is another kind of volunteer: the young man who volunteers for military service. He, of course, is paid a salary. His motives may be patriotism, an appetite for adventure, inability to succeed in civilian life, or a desire to avoid the less attractive consequences of waiting to be drafted. The Peace Corps Volunteer (PCV) is more like him than the other kind, mainly because he is paid a salary and mustering out pay. However, the Peace Corps, desiring to be identified with the other type of volunteer, refers to the money as a "living allowance."

"This allowance is not salary," says the *Peace Corps Fact Book and Directory*, "but is to cover the costs of adequate food, clothing, housing, utilities and incidentals such as laundry, tobacco, film and postage." The average world-wide living allowance in 1966 was $108 per month. There are also special clothing, travel, and settling-in allowances, plus the severance pay, which amounts to $1800 to $2000. Altogether, it is not much money, and most PCV's could make a great deal more in other jobs. But it is either propaganda or silliness not to call the living allowance a salary. The amount is set as the equivalent of that received as salary by indigenous personnel who do the same kind of work.

Thus, the so-called Volunteer is really a salaried employee of the United States government, paid in accordance with the wage standards customary in the country where the work is done. In some cases this is enough for bungalows, refrigerators, servants, and moderately gracious living. In others it is pretty grim. As in the army, there are good posts and bad ones.

Sargent Shriver, then U.S. Ambassador to France, told an audience in Cannes on September 9, 1968: "More than 100,000 have been in the Peace Corps working for nothing. Again, two years of their life for nothing, just to be of assistance to somebody." Of such hyperboles are credibility gaps manufactured.

If the Peace Corps is not really a peace corps, and the Volunteer is not really a volunteer, then what are these young people supposed to be? Their main purpose is ostensibly to provide what is called "middle level manpower" to developing nations. Middle-level manpower consists of those people who are not experts but who have professional-level competence in the skills that are needed for modernization and development. This includes teachers, mechanics, nurses, medical technicians, agronomists, plumbers, electricians, draftsmen, surveyors, etc. But as a matter of fact most PCV's do not have professional levels of competence. Instead they are college graduates without career job experience. In the Peace Corps they are called "A.B. generalists," and they far outnumber the declining number of professionals and blue collar workers. They are a highly select group, averaging about 24 years of age, totally unrepresentative of the part of the American population that makes the nation's decisions and does its work.

The numerical dominance of the Peace Corps by A.B. generalists came about by accident rather than design. In the early days Sargent Shriver and other Peace Corps officials held out hopes to the developing nations that they would be able to supply the skilled manpower that was most needed. Shriver traveled around the world advertising American capabilities and taking orders. He later discovered the hard reality that very few people with the needed skills were willing or able to disengage from their situations and go to work in a foreign country for Peace Corps wages. Moreover, some of those who did undertake such sacrifices were unable to acquire the linguistic skills or make the cultural adjustments necessary to their acceptance abroad. On the job they required more logistic support and handholding than the Peace Corps was able to give them. Therefore, because skilled workmen were too expensive to recruit and too costly to maintain, the Peace Corps increasingly leaned more heavily on the A.B. generalists. Whatever they lacked in professional competence, they presumably made up for in ease of recruitment, learning ability, tractability, and cultural adaptability.

It has generally been regarded in the Peace Corps that it is easier "to give the A.B. generalist a skill than to give sensitivity and the capacity for cultural understanding to the blue collar worker."[1] In 1967 the Peace Corps reported that less than three per cent of all Volunteers overseas were classified as doing blue collar work. Henry Norman, former Peace Corps Director in Guinea, believes that this is why countries that become irritated with the United States sometimes show their displeasure by throwing out the Peace Corps. It is dispensable, and they don't hurt themselves by getting rid of it. Norman bemoans the fact that the Peace Corps "has unwittingly molded itself from recruitment to termination in the image of the young liberal arts college graduate," and he calls for a more serious effort to recruit skilled workers.[2]

The predominance of A.B. generalists has fundamentally altered the character of the agency, for they simply do not constitute the kind and quantity of middle-level manpower that the Peace Corps was created to provide. Thus the needs expressed by the developing nations cannot be filled in the manner that they and the American public were originally led to believe. Moreover, if the process of development in these emerging nations is in fact being held up by the absence of such skilled manpower as the Peace Corps at first claimed, then is the Peace Corps really making any contribution to that development by sending A.B. generalists?

The Peace Corps Director in Togo, who had also served in Guinea, commented on this issue in 1968. Speaking of the experience in Guinea, he said: "For the most part A.B. generalists were recruited who were trained well on how to be good Volunteers but disastrously undertrained in the skills required for their jobs in Guinea. It was assumed that any good 'red blooded young American' coming from a highly sophisticated society could teach the peasants of the underdeveloped country something. I think this was a dangerous underestimation of the people we are dealing with in Africa . . . Unfortunately, the Guinea error has been repeated several times since 1963 . . . If we continue to send overseas Volunteers who are underskilled, we endanger ourselves and the Peace Corps with serious political consequences."[3]

About half of the PCV's are teachers, and despite the lack
of previous experience for most of them, it is clear that they
are making a contribution toward the improvement of education in many countries. To some degree, and this is not
really measurable, they, and the PCV's engaged in community development work, are affecting attitudes toward progress and self-help among the people with whom they work.
But the impact that this has on development is not as readily
apparent as the fact that the host countries would generally
prefer more skilled people and accept A.B. generalists primarily out of desperation or under the influence of U.S.
embassy salesmanship.

Nevertheless, the demand for whatever the Peace Corps
can provide, skilled or semi-skilled, is still greater than the
number of Volunteers it can put into the field. A decline in
qualified applicants forced Jack Vaughn in 1968 to scale
down by 2000 the number of planned Volunteers for 1969
and to increase the budget for recruiting by $109,000 to
$2.2-million.[4] An expanded campus recruitment effort oper-
ated out of four regional offices. It was based on a December,
1967, study by the Louis Harris polling organization of attitudes toward the Peace Corps held by 1000 college seniors,
on 50 campuses.[5]

According to a summary of the Harris survey published
in the *Peace Corps Volunteer*, there was a slight decline from
the previous year (from 16% to 13%) in the number of
seniors seriously considering the Peace Corps service. "The
biggest drop in interest," said the *Volunteer*, "was in the
most active group, especially among the 3-4 per cent classified as 'extreme activists.' Only 19 per cent of the extreme
activists were seriously considering the Peace Corps in December, compared with 40 per cent in 1966. Interest in the
most active group as a whole declined from 33 per cent in
1966 to 25 per cent." The Harris organization determined

activism on the basis of whether or not a senior had done, or
would do, any of the following: sign a petition, participate
in a demonstration, join a picket line, defy the school authorities, risk a future security clearance, violate the law, go to
jail, or participate in civil disobedience. "Most active"
seniors were those who had participated in at least four of
these.

The Harris study saw growing opposition to the Peace
Corps among activists as a potential danger. "If this opposition continues to grow," said the Harris study, "and the most
active group [on campus] continues to increase, interest in
the Peace Corps might be nibbled away from the left end of
the activity spectrum. . . . If this is to be avoided, the Peace
Corps must make it as clear as possible on the college
campuses that it is independent and offers the opportunity
for personal and effective involvement in the struggle to
improve society throughout the world."

Not only did the Harris survey confirm an observable
turning away from the Peace Corps by campus activists, it
suggested that those who do enlist are a special socio-economic group. "Generally," reported the *Volunteer*, "those
seriously considering the Peace Corps were least involved
with career or money pressures, the major reasons why other
students hesitated to join."

It is hazardous to generalize about the Volunteers, just
as it is risky to generalize about college students. Each is
an individual, and each is different. Nevertheless, there do
seem to be trends and tendencies. They show up in surveys
like that of Louis Harris and in the comments of those who
work with Volunteers, those who train them, and the Volunteers themselves.

As early as October, 1963, a controversy developed within
the Peace Corps over what the Director of the program in
Bolivia, Jasin Edwards, labeled the "bland volunteer." This

was the Volunteer who didn't cause many problems, but he didn't do anything very interesting or important either. Edwards felt that the Peace Corps was getting too many such people, and that they were a major problem. An increase in expulsions and drop-outs, both in training and overseas, also suggested to many that the quality of applicants was on the way down.[6]

Whether the problem was due to the quality of people who applied or to the criteria by which people were "de-selected," to use the Peace Corps euphemism, it is my opinion that the long term trend has been toward blandness and an apolitical kind of conformity among Volunteers. There are important exceptions, as I shall show, but in general the trend has been toward a Peace Corps composed of people who accept the world as the establishment describes it to them, and view their volunteering primarily as a device to help them find a suitable place in it. Without doubt the Peace Corps leadership has encouraged this with its adver-tising. "So you'll get to be President of U.S. Copper two years later," said a 1967 ad. "What's your hurry? You know everything you want to do will still be here to do in a couple of years. The only thing you don't know is what a couple of years in the Peace Corps will do for you. Maybe it'll help you get to be President of U.S. Copper faster. . . ."[7] This is hardly the campaign designed to recruit the idealist who wants to change the world, or the Black student who would simply laugh at the idea of "U.S. Copper" even giving him a decent job.

Until Jack Vaughn took over as Director there appeared to be a constant pressure within the Peace Corps bureaucracy toward greater tolerance of what came to be called the "high risk/high gain" type of Volunteer, that is, the unusual indi-vidual who might raise problems of one kind or another, but who might also achieve something spectacularly good. But

even under Shriver there were clearly limits, as was revealed in an incident with Otto Passman's House Subcommittee on Foreign Aid Appropriations. During the very first
hearings before Passmann's committee, Shriver was questioned about a newspaper account of an incident involving
a certain Charles Kamen who had been accepted for training.
Kamen had attended a meeting of the Miami Rotary Club
where the film *Operation Abolition* was shown. The film is
a grossly distorted attack on student opposition to the House
Committee on Un-American Activities. Kamen had allegedly
spoken out against the film at the meeting, and had been
ejected. Passman wanted to know whether such a person
would be allowed in the Peace Corps, and Shriver said that
he had asked the FBI to investigate the situation and did not
want to judge the case before the facts were in. Then there
was the following exchange with Representative J. Vaughan
Gary of Virginia:

Rep. Gary: ". . . Regardless of the other evidence, he
admits that he attended the meeting as a guest and attempted
to speak, and that was very indiscreet, if nothing more."

Mr. Shriver: "No question about it. It will weigh heavily
against him. There is no doubt about that."

Rep. Gary: "It shows a lack of judgment which you would
not want overseas, I would say."

Mr. Shriver: "Perhaps you are right."[8]

Seventy pages later in the hearings the issue came up
again. This time the questionner was Representative George
Andrews of Alabama.

Rep. Andrews: "Could we find out if he is a 'beatnik'?
I do not know what a beatnik is except I understand they
do not bathe or shave. . . . If we take people who have no
regard for their personal appearance in my opinion they
will detract from the attractiveness of your organization."

Mr. Shriver: "There is no question that such people will not be sent overseas."[9]

Two years later Rep. Passmann revealed what had happened to Charles Kamen. "I remember," he said, "an incident down in Miami. Certain people in your organization—you may have been one of them—were somewhat belligerent over the suggestion that you drop from your rolls this beatnik-type fellow who was removed bodily from a Rotary Club meeting. I had a call one night when we were marking up the bill and it was only then you let the man go. Those are some of the things that worry us about this organization."[10]

In response Sargent Shriver said: "In fact, this particular candidate that you were talking about was rejected by the selection people for service abroad without any intervention by the Director of the Peace Corps at all. Now, I think that the integrity of the selection process, which is not subject to political pressure or pressures of other types, is in the best interest of keeping good people in the Corps."[11]

There may indeed have been no intervention by the Director's office, or by other subordinates, and Kamen may have been eliminated for reasons having nothing to do with his opposition to the House Committee on Un-American Activities or whether or not he was a beatnik. But Shriver's response that the Peace Corps selection process was insulated from political pressure was not entirely convincing. Indeed, it appears that fear of political pressure is the principle reason why the Peace Corps insists that each Volunteer pass a full field investigation by the Civil Service Commission. If a PCV later turns out to be a Communist or a homosexual, the Peace Corps can blame another agency for not discovering it. But it is a costly procedure, both in money and in narrowing the base for recruitment, as testimony before the Senate Foreign Relations Committee in 1968 revealed. Chairman J. William Fulbright questioned Jack Vaughn and the Peace Corps legal counsel Michael Sharlot about the number of people removed each year as a result of the full field investigation, and Sharlot responded:

Mr. Sharlot: "I would say if there are 10 or 15 cases a year where a person is removed solely on the basis of information in the full field, it seems to me that is probably maximum."

Senator Fulbright: "Ten a year out of how many thousand would be how many?"

Mr. Sharlot: "Well, 8,000, let's say, 9,000. . . ."

Senator Fulbright: ". . . You spend $4 million on this exercise to find 10 men that are unacceptable; $400,000 is almost as much as we spend to kill a Vietcong. I don't see how you can justify this. . . . You are not going to destroy the Peace Corps if one or two get by. . . ."[12]

Later the Peace Corps submitted the following statement to be included in the record: "Approximately 2 percent of applicants who have accepted invitations to begin training for Peace Corps service have their invitations withdrawn or are deselected because the information in the full field investigation reports indicates they are clearly unsuitable or ineligible for volunteer service. In addition, the decision on the suitability of perhaps as much as 20 percent of Peace Corps trainees is, in substantial measure, aided by information contained in the full field investigation reports."[13]

It is simply impossible for an outsider to learn how this process works, and what quality of evidence is sufficient for exclusion. I have known several persons who claim they were dropped because of their political views, although other reasons were given them by the Peace Corps. Peace Corps officials reply that some individuals will allege political discrimination in order to conceal the real reasons which might be embarrassing. The Peace Corps, in order to protect the individuals concerned, does not make public the reasons for elimination, although the Volunteer may explain it any way he likes. This is a humane policy, but it does create uncertainty, particularly in the minds of potential Volunteers who have a record of campus activism.

Whatever the number of exclusions that specifically result from the full field investigations, this procedure undoubtedly affects recruitment in more subtle ways. There are many potentially valuable Volunteers who simply do not want their personal lives so thoroughly investigated and the results filed in Washington. Others with minor involvements in campus radicalism assume, perhaps incorrectly, that these will disqualify them, and do not apply. Such assumptions are hardly discouraged by such statements as the 1965 press release which said that "there is no place in the Peace Corps for beatniks, kooks, draft dodgers or their ilk." There are not many "high risk/high gain" types who have not been called names like that at one time or another.

In 1965 Deputy Director Warren Wiggins, Associate Director Harris Wofford, and Frank Mankiewicz, the Regional Director for Latin America (and later to become press secretary for Robert Kennedy's 1968 presidential primary campaign) launched a campaign to recruit more liberal-left political activists into the Peace Corps. "Strongly motivated people," Wiggins told the press, "with intense social and political convictions, might give us some trouble as individuals. But on the whole, their contribution to the program will be greater." Referring to peace and civil rights activists Wiggins said: "We would like to get some of the same dynamism and intellectual energy these young people display channeled into Peace Corps programs. We want people with a passion to make their world better, to take a stand and to make sacrifices. But obviously we don't want those who don't know where to draw the line, and who try to become political activists abroad."[14]

Frank Mankiewicz, generally regarded within the Peace Corps as a sort of resident revolutionary, even tried to recruit members of sds. "The things sds has done in Newark are valuable for our volunteers to be exposed to," said Mankiewicz. "We want to take advantage of their experience." [15] This was before the Newark riots of July, 1967.

The sds response was skeptical. "We're really open to this kind of move by the Peace Corps," said sds Executive Secretary Paul Booth, "but it shouldn't be just a move to get student radicals off the streets and shipped to Turkey, where they can't do any harm." [16]

Ultimately, this window to the left was never opened very wide, although a few radicals did join primarily to escape the draft. When in 1966 President Johnson appointed Jack Vaughn to replace Sargent Shriver, it was not long before Wiggins, Wofford, and Mankiewicz all left the Peace Corps, taking with them many of their most liberal and able subordinates. It was a major turning point.

Any agency which must try to look good to both the college campus and a reactionary congressional committee is in an extremely difficult, if not impossible, position. It can really accomplish this only by saying one thing to the congress and another to the students, a practice which eventually produces a credibility gap. The extent to which the Peace Corps does this is symbolized by the fact that some returned pcv's hired to recruit on college campuses wear beards, even though Jack Vaughn disapproved of them for Volunteers abroad. He is also selecting out Volunteers who, according to the full field investigation, have experimented with drugs and marijuana.

In the summer of 1968 the full field investigation of a Volunteer, then in training to go to Brazil, revealed the alleged use of marijuana. On those grounds he was dropped from the program. This so angered the other Volunteers that

they threatened, at the last minute, not to get on the plane
that was to take them to Brazil. Ultimately self-interest
triumphed, and they went. The suspended Volunteer ap-
pealed his case and was subsequently reinstated, but the drug
question continues to plague the Peace Corps because of the
extensive experimentation with marijuana and psychedelics
on college campuses. The policy of disqualifying Volunteers
who have "frequently" or "recently" used drugs has been
very difficult to administer.

The process of screening during training, called selection,
is one of the most controversial and, among Volunteers, trau-
matic aspects of the Peace Corps. It is understandable that a
government agency concerned with sending young people
overseas to represent the United States would want to find
out as early as possible whether an individual could adjust
to the hardship of the local environment, learn the language,
get along with the people he would have to work with, and
in general comport himself in a manner that would not bring
discredit upon the nation that sent him. Obviously the time
to find out these things is in training; hence selection.

The task is complicated and there was not much experience
on which to draw. Some studies had been made of the selection procedures used by the oss during World War II, and
the British had trained some people for overseas development work, but nothing exactly fitted Peace Corps needs. An
early decision was made to turn to the field of psychology
in order to develop screening procedures, and this discipline
consequently had a major impact on the character of the
Corps. During training Volunteers were given a battery of
psychological tests, interviews, and peer group ratings. These
procedures were then studied in order to determine which of
them were the best indicators of the subsequent performance
of the Volunteer in the field. It seemed like a properly scien-

tific way to go about the problem, and a great deal was learned as time went on.

But the selection process itself produced some unhappy reactions. The intensive interviewing began to look to the Volunteers very much like an invasion of privacy, and they resented it. They also recognized that in order to avoid being selected out, they had to play a role, they had to conform to the psychologists' notion of what constituted a mentally healthy, properly American, volunteer. Some training programs spawned rather well organized conspiracies to beat the system by feeding the "spies" the information that the Volunteers assumed the establishment wanted to hear.

One of the worst aspects of the selection procedures in the early days was the fact that the Volunteer had no way of knowing how he was doing until he was suddenly told he was in or out. This produced a high level of anxiety, a product which some of the selection people felt was beneficial in that it provided an opportunity to assess how an individual would behave under stress.[17] This was done in these ways: First, there was an intensive training schedule, typically running from 7 a.m. to 10 p.m. six days a week. Second, the Volunteers were required to write papers and perform other assignments during their "free time." Third, Volunteers were under intensive surveillance by instructors, dormitory leaders, and staff. Even remarks made over a beer could go into the files. Fourth, Volunteers had to submit to psychiatric interviews inquiring into their emotional stability, aggressiveness, and sexual orthodoxy. Those who deviated from an undefined norm were interrogated at greater length. Fifth, Volunteers were required to submit peer group ratings of their colleagues. Thus each became a judge and a potential accomplice to the expulsion of others. Sixth, Volunteers were required to pass certain tests showing a willingness to undertake difficult or frightening tasks. One of the most publicized by

the Peace Corps was "rapeling," the mountain-climbing technique, which Volunteers were asked to perform at the Puerto
Rico training center. It consisted of a high speed descent
down the sheer face of a cliff, sliding on a rope while pushing
the body away from the cliff with the feet.[18] The cumulative
effect of all these features was to produce an atmosphere
more akin to hazing, or to what a layman would expect James
Bond to have to endure, than an academic learning environment.

There was no shortage of critics of this approach, and the
Peace Corps Volunteer frequently printed letters about the
selection procedure. It did have its defenders, but the critics
seem to have dominated the dialogue. Fairly typical was a
letter written by L. Lloyd Morgan, a Volunteer in Tanzania.
"Indeed, with hindsight," wrote Morgan, "training seems to
be as much indoctrination of proper attitudes needed to be
'bland' as actual training for needed skills." He described
the training atmosphere as "neo-Orwellian," and said the
trainees referred to it as a "fishbowl." "The trainee is always
being watched. Even at parties the staff seems always to be
present." Morgan says that the Volunteer quickly learns to
"appear average, adjusted, well-liked, 'motivated'."[19]

Morgan's letter elicited an immediate response (in the
same issue of the *Volunteer*) from the Director of the Division of Selection, Al Carp. Carp reported on data derived
from questionnaires administered anonymously to 5000
trainees during the summer of 1965. He said that 65% felt
that selection had contributed significantly to selecting the
best trainees; only 15% disagreed. Seventy-eight per cent
said the atmosphere had either a positive effect or no effect.
Only 6% felt that the selection techniques were too personal.
Carp said that "training atmospheres such as Mr. Morgan
describes have existed in the past," but he said that the Peace
Corps was trying to "reduce this selection aura" by making

greater use of feedback and "self-selection."

Self-selection is Peace Corps jargon for the decision of a Volunteer to resign from training. It is a procedure which the Peace Corps encourages for those who discover through the training program that the life of a PCV is not likely to be their cup of tea. Self-selection is further evidence of the growing influence of psychology on the Peace Corps. Having been recruited primarily to, in the words of one of them, "prevent kooks from going overseas," the psychologists appear to be playing a major role in shaping the entire training experience. There are undoubtedly many reasons for this, some of which may be inferred from a talk to Field Assessment Officers by Gene Gordon, a senior psychiatric consultant. "Peace Corps Volunteers," he said, "are young people who do not know themselves very well, but they want to, very much. They wish to know themselves, to find out what they really want, to find their own thing is, in my opinion, the principal motivation for their joining the Peace Corps. . . . The Peace Corps is a detour which they have taken to find out who they are and what they want to do in life."[20]

It is a short leap from this analysis of Volunteer motivation to a conception of training as a process of self-discovery, emotional growth, and even psycho-therapy. In such a conception, the model Volunteer becomes one who confronts a personal crisis, and makes a mature decision. He does not ask the "therapist" to make it for him. He decides himself whether to go or not to go. And if the trainee senses no personal crisis, then the training program can be designed to produce one. Meanwhile the psychologists and the psychiatrists look on, and if the unsuitable trainee makes the "wrong" decision, they change it.

Gordon reported in 1968 that although great emphasis had been placed on self-selection, "nonetheless, even now in many programs the great expectation and the great fear is that selection is the ultimate responsibility of the FSO [Field Selection Officer] and FAO [Field Assessment Officer], both generally psychologists, and that they are going to exercise that responsibility, being witch doctors, in some arbitrary, capricious, esoteric manner to prevent perfectly normal American boys and girls from realizing their hearts desire. The consequent suspicion and mistrust which devolves on the psychologist and the psychiatrist is often monumental. And it is not only the Volunteers who feel this way; in many programs the degree of paranoia that develops among the staff about selection approaches the psychotic."

"I might say, in all frankness," Gordon continued, "that there is a grain of truth in these paranoid reactions. I cannot speak for the psychologists, but among several hundred psychiatrists who have worked for the Peace Corps in the past eight years, about a third were really perceptive, exciting, effective people; another third were very pedestrian, limited people and a remaining third can only be described as egregious boobs. Some of the arbitrary esoteric grounds on which people have been de-selected would make your hair curl; and conversely some of the blatantly crazy or psychopathic characters who have been blithely sent overseas would be equally appalling."[21]

A reading of an independent evaluation of a Peace Corps project in Peru prepared by members of the Cornell University Department of Anthropology will show that this is no exaggeration. It tells how one Volunteer, in a short period of time,

—assisted a Peruvian friend in castrating the friend's father's valuable stud donkey by a method which he called "the American style" and which resulted in the donkey hemorrhaging to death, the father punishing the son, and the son running away;

—promised to reimburse the owner for the donkey but did not do so;

—took over the club and game room of some Peruvian school teachers for use as a tack room for Peace Corps horses, until the teachers threw him out;

—hit a pedestrian while driving a truck but failed to report the accident;

—encouraged Peruvians who admired his musical ability to buy expensive instruments so that he could give them lessons, and then refused to teach them when he found out they wanted to play only local music.[22]

The question raised by all of this is not how do such persons (and the Cornell study describes others just as spectacular) get through selection. No system can be perfect. Neither is it a question of how to recruit more psychiatrists of the upper third type described by Dr. Gordon. There probably are not enough of them, and the Peace Corps could not afford them if there were. The issue is whether the Peace Corps is over-emphasizing "psycho-dynamics" at the expense of professionalism in the middle level manpower skills that the emerging nations really need, and whether its pressure cooker training, even in its current, less vigorous form, is deterring good people from joining the Peace Corps, and causing others to "de-select" themselves. Questionnaires answered by 5000 trainees who adjusted to this procedure and survived it could hardly shed light on these questions.

From the beginning, two tendencies have coexisted in uneasy tension within the Peace Corps. One tendency may be described as professionalist. It is advanced by those people who view the Peace Corps as an aid to development, who regard development as requiring professional skills, who see the mission of the Peace Corps as providing those skills so that measurable results can be obtained.

The other tendency can be quite appropriately labeled the

Dale Carnegie approach—how to win friends and influence people in the developing countries. This means being personally liked and projecting a good image of Americans in general. The term used in training Volunteers for the Philippines is "S.I.R.", smooth interpersonal relations, but some variant of it is emphasized for all the countries where the Peace Corps operates.

Obviously, any effort by foreigners to encourage development and modernization requires a mixture of these two approaches. You cannot teach necessary skills if you are not professional, and the local people will not learn from you if they do not like, or at least, trust you. The problem is to keep these tendencies in proper balance.

By 1965 the Peace Corps appeared to be achieving an effective balance in its selection techniques, but the social and political climate of America did not permit much to come of it. Primarily because of the Vietnam war, but also because of experimentation with drugs and the hippie way of life, the attitudes of American young people, particularly on college campuses, began to change radically. The Peace Corps' notion of the life style of a proper Volunteer became more and more remote from what was developing on the campuses where recruitment had been most successful. As the colleges became more radical, the Peace Corps drifted more toward the Dale Carnegie approach to selection, particularly after Vaughn replaced Shriver. The cause of this, in my opinion, was not the anthropologists who taught the trainees how to "go native" or the psychologists who tried to remove those whose psyches could not withstand the resulting "culture shock."

The root cause was political. It had to do with the sort of instrument the Congress, the White House, and the Director wanted the organization to be. As I have shown in Chapter IV, the purpose of the Peace Corps is to advance the interests of the United States by making friends for America abroad. The training and selection process is designed to serve these ends by screening out those who will make a bad impression, and by helping the others to adjust.

In an information circular on the selection process, the Peace Corps tells the trainees that they will need to make adjustments to many frustrations when they get out on the job. "You will find a scarcity of tangible rewards," it says. But the Volunteer must persevere. "In a very real sense," the circular continues, "a Volunteer is expected to be able to do his best twenty-four hours a day, whatever the conditions may be, and in spite of negligible results." In other words do not expect results, just be a beautiful Volunteer, twenty-four hours a day. It is a logical posture for the representative of a foreign policy which is not really committed to developing the underdeveloped areas, but which is designed to maintain United States access and influence there. In this context, the Peace Corps is a form of international tokenism designed to pacify people, rather than change the conditions that cause their misery.

During the bland Volunteer controversy a PCV stationed in Tanzania wrote to the *Peace Corps Volunteer* describing how her training program had screened out and pressured the non-conformists. She also sent in the words of a song some of the trainees had sung:

> *We are marching in formation*
> *Down the middle of the road*
> *For to turn to either left or right*
> *Is dangerous, we're told;*
> *Sargent Shriver wants his teachers*
> *Always docile, never bold,*
> *And the Peace Corps marches on.*
> *Glory, glory mediocrity . . .*

It is, of course, not as bad as that. If it were, one could

dismiss the Peace Corps as an instrument of American foreign policy. In fact, what the Peace Corps has produced is a reasonably bright, attractive group of middle-class young people, some of whom make a very good impression on the local inhabitants whether they accomplish anything or not. They are not too idealistic, certainly not radical, and they do not worry much about politics. They are other-directed and practical, not profound. They are the twentieth century equivalents of the young civil servants of the British East India Company, the American "competition wallahs" who take their examinations, endure their hazing, train in their Haileybury Colleges, and then go off to take upon their shoulders, ever so gracefully, the white man's burden.

VI: PACIFICATION

"One of the fastest-growing activities in U.S. guerrilla programs is the use of military units to take on civic action projects in underdeveloped nations. The theory is that guerrillas can operate successfully only when the civilians are in sympathy with them. To win loyalty from native populations and make guerrilla warfare less likely, Air Commandos and Special Forces help truck drinking water into slum areas of Guayaquil, Ecuador, fly medical teams into rural Bolivia, build roads and schools in the Dominican Republic. Most such projects are in Latin America. . . .

"Roughly 3,000 residents around the isolated village of Chiman in Panama's south coast recently were startled to hear a voice from an airplane loudspeaker: 'Good morning, friends of Chiman. This is a Commando aircraft of the U.S. Air Force. Mr. Mayor, all towns that have an airfield are able to carry their products to market more quickly and in case of emergency are able to receive assistance promptly. We are able to help you build an airfield if you would like one.' Commando planes dropped two strips of luminous orange tape and then instructions to Chiman to make, if it assented to this proposition, an 'X' from the stuff on the ground. Next day, the 'X' was there. Commandos flew in all the equipment needed to build the strip, watched villagers complete it in two months from instructions dropped or broadcast entirely from the air."

"U.S. Guerrillas: With Knife and Strangling Wire," *Time*, May 24, 1963.

When President Johnson signed the 1965 Peace Corps Act he addressed some remarks to the Volunteers. "I wish," he said, "there were as many of you as there are soldiers, sailors and marines. The more we have of you, the less we will need of them."[1]

To the President, this comment may simply have been one of those flattering platitudes that politicians feel they must utter on occasions such as this. But whether it was intended or not, the comment is quite correct in suggesting that the Peace Corps does the work which otherwise might have to be done by the military services. Only the methods are dif-

ferent, and even in this regard, there are some striking
similarities.

The greatest threat to continued U.S. expansion in the
developing areas is the possibility of revolutions which would
nationalize foreign-owned enterprises and place severe restrictions on foreign investments. The extreme examples of
such revolutions are, of course, the Chinese and the Cuban,
but other countries have also severely limited foreign economic penetration. It is one of the primary aims of American
foreign policy to prevent such developments, and the Department of Defense has spent great amounts of money for re-
search on revolutionary movements and techniques for con-
trolling them.

A lesson apparently learned from Vietnam is that if revolutions are to be prevented, and certainly if they are to be
prevented without great expenditures, then action must be
taken early. Revolutionary movements must be detected at
the earliest possible times and contained, deflated, co-opted
or liquidated.

In the developing countries of Asia, Africa, and Latin
America, revolutions, if they occur, are most likely to be born
in the universities, in the urban slums, and among peasants
in the countryside. It is of course possible for revolutions
to start in the trade unions, where they exist, or in the army,
as in Egypt. But these are less common. Destroying them
early requires, first of all, knowing that they are developing.
This means good intelligence—knowing what is going on in
the barrios, the remote villages, and among the students.
What are people thinking? Are they discontented with the
existing government? Are there leaders among them who
are capable of building mass movements? Are there reforms
which could be made which would placate the population and
lower the revolutionary potential?

It is, of course, essential for the existing government of

a given country to know these things if it is to avoid a revolution. It is similarly important for the United States government to have this knowledge in order to determine the kind
and level of economic and military assistance necessary to
enable the local government to cope with the situation.

Revolution is related to alienation, and if revolution is to
be prevented, then something must be done about alienation
before it reaches the point where revolutionaries can exploit
it. A way must be found to give people a sense of identification with their government, and a feeling that it is possible
to make progress within the existing governmental system.
In the countryside this means that someone must go among
the people, live with them, work with them, help them, and
provide personal evidence that someone in authority cares.

The more capable administrators in British India understood this, and knew how to do the job. The history of British
rule is replete with stories of individual British civil servants
cementing a bond between the system and thousands of
Indians. One example goes back to the eighteenth century
and the time of Warren Hastings when the East India Company was having great difficulties maintaining law and order
among certain aboriginal tribes. One group, the Sauria Pa-
harias, were known as marauding savages, and even stern
military reprisals by the Muslim government had not been
able to subdue them. They were finally pacified by one
Englishman, Augustus Clevland. According to one account:

"The secret of his success was simply that he conciliated
and won the confidence of a wild people. He went among
them unarmed, presided at their tribal feasts, respected and
preserved the authority of their chiefs, encouraged agriculture and started markets for the sale of their produce. Clevland has accordingly been generally, and also officially,
credited with being the originator of the policy of making
aboriginal tribes the agents of their own civilization and of

turning their spears into plowshares by moral suasion rather than by force. . . . The memorial of the East India Company submitted in 1858 . . . stated that he was the first person who was known to have tried the effect of justice and conciliation on any of the hill tribes and recorded the interesting fact that the feelings which he left behind among the ruder people of the district were such, that they long continued to pay religious honors to his tomb."[2]

Clevland died in 1784 at the age of twenty-nine. Warren Hastings himself erected a tomb which bore an inscription telling how Clevland "without bloodshed or the terror of authority, employing only the means of conciliation, confidence and benevolence, attempted and accomplished the entire subjection of the lawless and savage inhabitants of the Jungleterry of Rajamahall, who had long infested the neighboring lands by their predatory incursions, inspired them with a taste for the arts of civilized life and attached them to the British government by a conquest over their minds— the most permanent as the most rational mode of dominion."[3]

Another example of the relationship between good works and governmental control is the achievement of the Deputy Commissioner of Firozpur in Punjab:

"Colonel [then Captain] Grey had no funds nor expert staff beyond two surveyors lent by the Bahawalpur State, where he had already started an irrigation system; but he succeeded in getting thirteen canals constructed, and over a quarter of a million acres irrigated, without Government having to spend a penny. He succeded by reason of his influence with the people of the district, whom he induced to work on a cooperative system operating on a huge scale. The canals were designed by Colonel Grey; the work, including vast excavation and the construction of dams and embankments, sluices and aqueducts, was carried out by the people, whom he taught and supervised. It meant immense labor for

Colonel Grey and his Assistant . . . for, in addition to ordinary revenue and judicial duties, they themselves worked
with chain and tape, teaching an improvised staff how to
survey, superintended the actual work of construction, and
toiled with the people in the repair of breeches made by
floods—on one occasion for eighteen hours on end. Colonel
Grey had his reward in the gratitude of the people, as well as
in the knowledge that he had spread plenty over a smiling
land. . . . Till at least thirty years afterwards his praises
were sung in popular songs with the refrain 'All praise to
Grey Sahib. Never will there be another like him'." [4]

The kind of work and the rapport toward the people demonstrated by Clevland and Grey is virtually identical to what
is done by many Peace Corps Volunteers today. The major
difference, of course, is that Clevland and Grey had administrative authority. PCV's are not officials of either the host
government or the American government. They are not magistrates, tax collectors, or policemen. But in some cases this
difference may be more formal than real, and the Peace Corps
may in fact be performing certain governmental functions
which the government is unable or unwilling to perform for
itself. In some cases, Peace Corps assumption of governmental functions is quite obvious, as in Liberia, for example.
According to a 1968 recruitment brochure entitled *The Peace
Corps and Liberia:*

"Twenty-five Volunteers are also employed in 11 government administrative agencies. They are working side by side
with Liberians demonstrating skills and techniques in public
administration. Three Volunteers are working under the supervision of county superintendents, helping to ensure the
success of President Tubman's unification program. They
are *doers*, not advisors. By actually demonstrating modern
administrative techniques, they are bringing Liberia's goal

of viable, self-sufficient nationhood a little closer." (Emphasis in original)

The 1969 program directory describes plans to recruit more Volunteers who will go to Liberia and "study present rules and regulations in government agencies, work out ways for putting suggested improvements into action, and recommend methods of using techniques and assistance available to Liberia from international agencies and private foundations." The directory says that in this way Volunteers can "play a crucial role in developing an efficient government administration in Liberia."

The drift toward governmental decision-making, as opposed to purely economic development work, can also be seen in the Peace Corps program in Micronesia, where in the summer of 1968 there were 650 Volunteers in service, one Volunteer for every 138 Micronesions.[5] In the previous June one of these Volunteers wrote an article for the *Peace Corps Volunteer* which was an appeal for the Corps to accept a greater administrative role. "In Micronesia," he wrote, ". . . several Volunteers have rapidly become administrators of needed development programs. They are professionals . . . responsive to the people served by the programs and cognizant of their affiliation with those people. More broadly, this means a Peace Corps of development-oriented Volunteers whose ultimate value lies in decision-making, not in the fact that they live at the people's level and could easily remain there as impotent Volunteer empathizers. . . . Just as many villagers who know the Volunteer may vocally desire that the Volunteer become the local government official, so in this extended professional corps the Volunteer administrator can attempt to approximate the idea of a professional whose knowledge and affiliation still lies with the people served."[6]

Micronesia is a trust territory administered by the United States, and Liberia is a semi-colony dominated by American interests. It is not surprising, therefore, that this drift toward governmental functions can be seen most clearly there. But there are imperatives which impel Volunteers in this direction no matter where they work—the desire for efficiency, and the elimination of red tape being the most important. Wherever local government is weak, Volunteers unconsciously may move in subtle ways into the vacuum.

I am not suggesting either that this is the formal, articulated policy of the Peace Corps, or the conscious intent of the Volunteers. Where strength is placed in competition with weakness, it usually tends to dominate. One Volunteer— healthy, intelligent, knowledgeable, sympathetic—placed among ignorant, impoverished, helpless people, can exert influence of extraordinary proportions. In a colony or semi-colony this influence gravitates toward administration; in an independent country it is simply political.

The Peace Corps work which puts Volunteers in such situations is called Community Development. This concept is a matter of continual discussion within the Peace Corps, and officially it has never been precisely defined. However, a good description of the work done by a community developer is given in the 1968 recruitment pamphlet *What Can I Do in the Peace Corps?* The pamphlet lists the following activities:

• "To study his community and its people so that he understands their interests and is aware of their stage of development.

• "To identify the felt needs of the people as well as other needs.

• *"To establish and maintain cordial and constructive relationships with government officials and other members of the power structure.*

• *"To promote the participation of all in the problem*

analysis and decision-making process through democratic procedures.

• "To help the people consider all aspects of a question; to plan and to implement a project and to evaluate the consequences of the decisions and actions they undertake.

• "To maintain a neutrality and objectivity in the face of pressures and factions and yet *remain accessible to all.*

• *"To stay in the background and yet be available for advice and reinforcement of positive and constructive ideas and moves.*

• "To help the people take the lead but *recognize the moment when it becomes necessary to assume temporary leadership.*

• "To be familiar both with government and private sector resources and services.

• "To seek and help the people use available technical advice.

• "To help technicians relate to the people of the community so that their technical advice is dispensed in an acceptable and usable manner.

• *"To stimulate and train leaders:* To encourage responsibility and planning, use of local abilities and talent; *to encourage and spur on; to warn and advise."* (Emphasis added)

I have italicized the functions which seem to me likely to put the Volunteer in an influential political position. Obviously, the distinction between the kind of leadership and manipulation necessary to achieve economic development, and that necessary to achieve political control is a fine one. In some developing societies the line between them is so fine as to be indistinguishable for both the Peace Corps Volunteers and the local population as well. An excellent example of the subtle relationship between politics and good community development work is the case of Rhoda and Earle Brooks, husband and wife Volunteers who served in the city

of Manta in Ecuador from 1962 to 1964. They are as close
to a perfect Peace Corps couple as one could imagine, a fact
not missed by the *National Geographic* magazine that featured
Rhoda on the cover for its Peace Corps story of September,
1964.

In 1961 the Brooks had graduated from college and held
paying jobs. He was twenty-eight and a sales engineer, and
she was a twenty-six year old school teacher. They had both
been interested in foreign students while in college, and
Rhoda had even planned to become a missionary in Africa.
When the formation of the Peace Corps was announced, they
immediately wrote a rather starry-eyed letter to President
Kennedy, offering their services.

In Manta the Brooks undertook a number of projects, some
of which were quite successful. They helped clear the streets
of garbage, and found a way to provide community garbage
cans. They gave health instruction, and did a variety of
other teaching jobs. They lived in the poorest sector of the
town and the people apparently adored them. To many of
them, the Brooks were the first people they had ever met from
the developed world. At the end of their tour of duty, they
adopted two local children, one the illegitimate offspring of
a rather scarlet woman, the other the child of a loving, but
overly large, family. Thus the ties with Ecuador were made
intensely personal and lasting.

The Brooks have described their two years in Manta in a
well-written and interesting book, *The Barrios of Manta* (New
York: New American Library, 1965). Their story is warm
and extremely touching. It is also an important revelation
of the political role of Volunteers, particularly because it
suggests that the Brooks were completely unaware of the
political significance of what they did. They certainly did
not see themselves as political agents. Nevertheless, they

did play an important role as propagandists and sources of intelligence.

The first important propaganda exercise came when the Ecuadorian government seized two United States fishing boats on the grounds that they were poaching on Ecuadorian territorial waters, then extending to two hundred miles.

"The Communists in Manta," Earle Brooks wrote, "passed out handbills almost daily—and they all said 'Yankee pirates go home.' People besieged us with questions, asking for an explanation of the United States violation of Ecuador's laws. We had to admit that our boats were legally in the wrong, but tried to suggest delicately that the two-hundred mile limit was extreme.

* * *

"My English conversation class, held between the morning and afternoon sessions of the high school, often got involved in discussions of communism and democratic capitalism. . . . My students were serious and sometimes the discussion ran for hours—quite a drain on my Spanish. . . ."

The Brooks then began to invite students and non-students to their home for "just talk."

"About fifteen young people came that first time. Some of them talked with an air of authority and several were very anti-American, but the discussion indicated their real lack of information about our democratic system of government. To many of them 'capitalist' was synonymous with murderer.

"We showed some slides of the United States that we had thrown into our trunks at the last minute; and we talked about United States wages, taxes, public schools, hospitals, social security, employment compensation, and unions, as well as of everyday life—entertainment, dating, family structure, sports, and religion."

The Brooks got many tough questions, but they said that "telling the truth about our weaknesses seemed to win their

admiration." Before the sessions, many of the participants
had thought "all North Americans were unfriendly," but the
pleasant demeanor of the Brooks demolished that stereotype.

The Brooks were not the only North Americans in Manta.
There were others, but they did not mix with poor Ecuadorians, and the Volunteers saw them infrequently. One
exception, however, was Bob Carpenter, the manager of the
Van Camp tuna packing plant in Manta. He approached the
Brooks as soon as they arrived in town, befriended them,
and even loaned them money. They described him as "an
unforgettable man" of considerable charm. He liked them,
and made a ritual of visiting them on Sunday mornings to
hear what they had been doing and exchanging gossip. "We
let ourselves go with Bob," said Rhoda, "he was a wonderful
listener and an outlet for our English which lay dormant
most of the week."

When the Arosemena government was overthrown, the new
regime abolished the two hundred mile limit, a matter which
might have been of some concern to citizens of a fishing town
like Manta. The authorities also arrested a young Communist
leader named Stalin Valdivieso, who had been to the home
of the Brooks for discussions. In jail, Valdivieso smuggled
out a note to the Brooks saying he was disillusioned with
Communism and asked their help in securing his release.
Earle describes what happened:

"It was the most ticklish situation of our two years in
Manta. I talked it over with Bob Carpenter, and he suggested
that this might be a good opportunity to get some information
from Stalin about the Communist party in exchange for his
freedom. I was glad the matter was out of my hands.

"Three days later Stalin and his two sisters, all dressed
up, appeared at our Thursday recreation night. With tears
in his eyes, he thanked me for helping him. I told him that
I had not arranged for his release but that I was glad to see

him free. 'In a Communist country,' I said to him seriously,
'you would have disappeared from sight and never been seen
again. You can be thankful that your country is guided by
men who have a sense of justice.'

"Shortly afterward, caches of arms were discovered and a
Communist plan to take over Ecuador was uncovered. The
exposure of this plot relieved most people, since Ecuador did
not want to be another Cuba. Most people felt that the military junta was just and was bringing about necessary reforms. . . . We had to admit that the methods of the junta
were superior to Arosemena's."

Earle tells how several months later three top military leaders visited a commercial fair in Manta where the Brooks
manned a booth. Theirs was the only booth of about fifty
that the dignitaries stopped to visit. They were very cordial,
and asked many questions. "Later that week," Earle writes,
"we received first prize for the Casa del Obrero exhibit and
public recognition from the consejo for our work and our
contributions to Manta's betterment."

There are certain things that are quite obvious from this
book. One is that the Brooks were very effective propagandists, showing USIA films one moment, holding political
discussions at another. They were also an important conduit
for political information. Whether Carpenter made a habit
of passing along what they told him during his regular visits,
or did so only in the one instance when Stalin was jailed, is
impossible to say. But it is clear that a competent intelligence agent, either of the Ecuadorian government or the CIA,
by bugging the Brooks house or by pumping either the Brooks
or Carpenter, could have learned much about what was
going on in Manta. Done with skill, the Brooks would never
have suspected, and would continue to see themselves simply
as agents of enlightenment and change.

It is also clear that the Brooks served to make the new

military junta more acceptable to the population. And finally, and most important from an American point of view, they helped make acceptable the change in territorial waters which enabled United States fishermen to move in and catch fish otherwise reserved for Ecuadorians.

Taken all together the Brooks did a remarkable job for the United States. It was done with good will and a sincere desire to help the people of Ecuador. But the significance of their work was not its contribution to economic development, which was certainly minimal, but to what can only be described as pacification—the prevention of unrest and the preservation of a climate conducive to law and order.

A man who certainly understood well how this works was the head of the Peace Corps. In 1968 Jack Vaughn, then the Corps' Director, was questioned about pacification by Representative Julia Hansen of the House Appropriations Committee.

Rep. Hansen: "How many Peace Corps people do you have working in the pacification program in Vietnam?"

Mr. Vaughn: "We have never been requested to provide them."

Rep. Hansen: "Why?"

Mr. Vaughn: "I don't know. My philosophy is that Peace Corps work is not an instrument of pacification after hostilities have started. Instead, volunteers are people who can work on the cause of hostilities.

*   *   *

"My position on the war in Vietnam is that if we some years ago had a Peace Corps there we would not be in the situation we now are. Our work in 57 countries will greatly help avoid Vietnams in the future." [7]

Vaughn apparently derived his attitudes about the effectiveness of the Peace Corps in pacification from his own experience in the State Department, and as Ambassador to

Panama where, he says, "I visited Volunteers constantly."
He also observed the effects of Peace Corps pacification in
Bolivia, about which he said:

"I've seen a lot of strange things. But I've never seen anything like what I saw in Bolivia a few days ago. I had been
stationed in Bolivia a couple of times and had left there last
in mid-1958. . . . I [had] reached the point where I was
reluctant to go up on the high plains near Lake Titicaca . . .
because of the menacing, hostile attitude of the Indians.
They were all armed, they seemed resentful, didn't speak
Spanish and didn't change. That was seven or eight years
ago.

"I visited five villages in that very same area in 1965. In
all five I was carried into town on the backs of the Indians
who wanted to show me that they were in the human race.
They had all built a school, the first school in a thousand
years. They all had potable water piped in, and they had
done it themselves. They had made more physical progress
in a couple years than they had made in the previous thousand. But more important was the attitude, the openness,
the willingness to look you in the eye and tell you about who
they were and what they had done, and the pride and self-
respect of citizenship. This was done by the Peace Corps . . .
in about three years. This is real revolution." [8]

Obviously, this was not revolution at all, but pacification.
The configuration of political power had not changed. Instead, the hostility of the population had diminished, and
the people had acquired "the pride and self-respect of citizenship."

Vaughn is concerned with pacification, not only in the rural
areas, but in the schools and universities as well, for it is
there that revolutionary leadership, particularly in Latin
America, is generally spawned. In 1965 when Vaughn was
the Assistant Secretary of State for Inter-American Affairs,

a subcommittee of the House Committee on Foreign Affairs was holding hearings on Communism in Latin America. Vaughn was invited to testify. His testimony was as fascinating as it was cryptic because of security deletions:

Mr. Vaughn: "I would like to start, Mr. Chairman, by telling you what I think is the central dilemma that we face, not only in Latin America, but around the world. It is this. [Security deletion.]"

Rep. Bolton: "Does that happen?"

Mr. Vaughn: "[Security deletion.] This is the problem we face. [Security deletion.]

"We are up against full-time Communist professionals when we have part-time, to a large extent, amateurs, combating communism. The battle has been going on for a long time. For example [security deletion] . . . they began to teach at universities and normal schools. [Security deletion.] We can say the recorded history of this effort of penetration and subversion begins in 1937, 1938, 1939. It has continued. They have been willing to play for the long pull, to infiltrate. They have a standard pattern. They go to the communications media. They go to the educational system. They go to the labor unions. They go to the judiciary. And they are willing to play a waiting game, and at the right time they come out. [Security deletion.]

* * *

"As far as the institutions in Latin America that have been influenced by communism, I think the main problem continues to be the university and normal schools. This has been a haven, because of their autonomous nature, because of the persuasion of many of the young intellectuals, and because of the heavy emphasis the Communists have given to these institutions. We have [security deletion] universities in Latin America, that are a constant threat, a production line for young Communists." [9]

That same month Vaughn addressed a conference of returned Peace Corps Volunteers in Washington. It was clear
from his speech that he was enormously impressed by the
Corps' political role in preventing the kind of class antago-
nisms that lead to revolution:

"I feel, in all sincerity, that the Peace Corps operation in
Panama means more to us, to you as taxpayers and to our
foreign policy, than all the tens of millions of dollars that
the United States Government has invested in Panama through
construction, technical grants and related projects under the
Alliance for Progress and predecessor agencies. . . .

"The Peace Corps has profound political merit as a force
for integration. . . . I have been surprised with how little the
Foreign Service Officer and the AID and USIA technicians know
of the countries in which they serve. The Peace Corps Volunteer works very effectively as an integrationist, putting in
contact, for the first time, people who haven't known each
other: the middle class with the upper class and the Salva-
dorian with the Costa Rican and the city dweller with the
rural dweller. This is a major contribution and I have seen
this happen hundreds of times.

"We have a lot to accomplish in Latin America in the
coming months and years. I don't think we can accomplish
any of it unless there is improved communications between
Latins themselves and between the classes. I see this as the
stellar role of the Peace Corps, the superb role that the Volunteers played in the country where I have been accredited for
the past ten months." [10]

It is evident from these quotations that Vaughn perceived
the main tasks of American foreign policy in Latin America
to be the integration of the most likely pro-American classes
(the middle and upper), and opposition to Communist influence in the Universities. These statements were made in
March, 1965. The following October, the same House sub-

committee that heard Vaughn held hearings on the work of the Peace Corps in Latin America, and Frank Mankiewicz, Regional Director for Latin America (Vaughn's old job), and Paul Bell, the Corps man in charge of the West Coast Division of Latin America, testified on the role of the Peace Corps in the universities:

Mr. Bell: ". . . We are quite interested in the universities because then we come into contact with the university students who are always so prone to strikes and other things."

Rep. Selden: "Are you getting more Peace Corps personnel into the universities? . . ."

Mr. Mankiewicz: "Yes, we are. I think in some countries we may have reached the point where we had better level off, but in other countries we are increasing the number of volunteers teaching in universities, and I think they are doing a very effective job.

*   *   *

"The United States uses a number of techniques and there are a number of ways in which Americans teach in Latin American universities. There are Fulbright scholars. There are exchange professors. They do not reach the number of universities or the kinds of universities in most cases that Peace Corps Volunteers do. In many countries regional and provincial universities really are universities only because they are called universities. But they are important places to be because this is where the emerging leadership of these countries is presently being educated. We are able to have a considerable impact."[11]

Mankiewicz went on to point out that it is the custom in Latin America not to have many full time professors. Most of the professors are lawyers and other professionals who teach one or two courses at the university. As a result they do not have a very intensive contact with the students on a day to day basis. The Peace Corps teachers, on the other hand, teach full time. "It makes an attractive situation," said Mankiewicz, "where they teach a class and then sit around after the class and talk to the class and have an interest in them, perhaps go down to the plaza and have a cup of coffee with them and perhaps even invite some of them for dinner. It is fairly common with U.S. professors, but it is practically unknown in Latin American universities. In that way we are making a considerable impact." [12]

It seems to me clear from the evidence that I have assembled that the work of the Peace Corps in community development and in education is of considerable propaganda and intelligence value, and that its central thrust is pacification or revolution prevention. Still it must be kept in mind that this is probably not the conscious aim of most volunteers or of most Peace Corps bureaucrats.

My own experience in helping to train several groups of volunteers, my correspondence and discussions with others, and reports of my former students who served in the Peace Corps lead me to believe that most Volunteers are apolitical, and many are very naive. It never occurs to most of them that they might be serving an intelligence or propaganda function. And the observations of many of them would be worthless. On the other hand there are a few who consciously seek a political role. The professional anti-Communist, Fred C. Schwarz, of the Christian Anti-Communism Crusade sent out a fund raising appeal on August 5, 1968 which quoted a letter received from a Volunteer in Colombia. The letter asked for 500 to 1000 copies of the Spanish edition of Schwarz's book for which the Volunteer said there was a "great potential need." Schwarz said the books were on their way.

Other Volunteers have applied to the Central Intelligence Agency for jobs, saying that their knowledge of foreign countries would make them valuable agents. Strictly speaking, this is forbidden by the Peace Corps; no volunteer is supposed to be employable by the CIA until he has been out of the Corps five years. President Kennedy laid down this rule in a telephone call to the Director of the CIA; it was later formalized in what is referred to as the "Helms Letter." [13] I discussed this question with Warren Wiggins, who was in charge of policing the agreement until he left the Peace Corps in 1966, and he was confident that it had been scrupulously observed. Letters from Volunteers to the CIA were, he assured me, turned over to the Peace Corps. Jack Vaughn told the House Appropriations Committee in 1968 that in one case the Volunteer was brought back and dropped from the Corps within twenty-four hours. [14] Wiggins would not tell me the number of such cases, but responded affirmatively when I asked if it was more than a dozen.

Volunteers who see themselves as agents or propagandists appear to be in the minority, and I see no reason to doubt the Peace Corps when it says that it shuns any formal relationship with the intelligence community and takes every possible precaution to prevent penetration.

However, Volunteers need have no affiliation with the CIA in order to play an intelligence role, as the experience of the Brooks in Manta clearly demonstrates. Volunteers customarily discuss their work and the situation in their areas with Peace Corps representatives who confer regularly with the American ambassador and other embassy officials. The Volunteers, therefore, constitute a network of eyes and ears that is indirectly in the service of U.S. policy makers. They are not trained intelligence gatherers, but they do know a great deal about the local affairs which are so important in predominantly rural countries.

Frank Mankiewicz has said that PCV's in Peru go about their jobs by first asking a lot of questions in the community: "What makes it tick? Who has the real power? How is

decision-making carried out? What are the physical resources, in terms not only of buildings, markets, stores,
schools, churches, but also of tools, education, and potential
leadership?"[15] Answers to such questions constitute valuable
intelligence, regardless of the motives whereby they were
secured. It is particulary important for governments to
identify emerging leadership, to compile dossiers, to know
how individuals may be influenced and what weaknesses they
may have. A good intelligence agent could get a considerable
amount of such information out of some Volunteers through
a "chance" meeting in a local bar.

Similarly, the Volunteer need not see himself as a policeman or soldier in order to be an effective agent of pacification. The line between community development and pacification is not distinct, and indeed the United States military
services are in some areas of the world behaving as if they
were themselves a peace corps. One of the best examples is
the Air Force Civic Action Unit, the 606th Air Commando
Squadron, formed in early 1966 for deployment in Thailand.
Military civic action is defined by the Air Force as "the use
of preponderantly indigenous military forces on projects
useful to the local populace at all levels in such fields as
education, training, public works, agriculture, transportation, communications, health, sanitation and others contributing to economic and social development which would also
serve to improve the standing of the (indigenous) military
forces with the population."[16]

The Air Force emphasizes that the key word in this defini-
tion is "indigenous," that its mission is to get the local people
to do the work. "The objective of the Americans in this program," writes an Air Force Captain in *The Airman*, "is to
work themselves out of a job."[17] "We firmly believe," says
Major Joe T. Williams, USAF, and Lt. Colonel Thomas P.
Griffin, USAF, "that our concept of advice, assistance, instruc-

tion, and limited logistical support for host country representatives in existing and established programs is a formidable weapon in the struggle against insurgency."[18] The Air
Force Commandos differ from the Peace Corps primarily in
that they work with the host country military, whereas the
Peace Corps Volunteers work with civilan agencies. Also the
Commandos do not live for extended periods in the villages,
but move around from place to place. But like the Peace
Corps the Commandos go into the villages unarmed and in
civilian clothes, and the work they do is very similar to Peace
Corps work. In Thailand they concentrate on medical aid,
veterinary services, and dentistry. In 1968 the Seventh Air
Force (Southeast Asia) reported that in one month MEDCAP
teams (medical civic action program) treated 12,456 medical
patients and 2,054 dental cases. They also give instruction
to villagers in modern techniques of livestock disease prevention, artificial insemination, and other skills useful to a
rural population. "Another area of endeavor," write Williams and Griffin, "in improving the socio-economic situation
of the rural Thai has been our efforts to develop a poultry
industry to provide fresh eggs to the United States Air Force
in up-country Thailand. Each poultry producer who improves his economic standing and the standard of living of
his family becomes an effective barrier (the first line of
defense) against insurgency propaganda." Presumably under
such a program, everybody benefits except the Communists
and the chickens. U.S. soldiers get fresh eggs, Thai farmers
make some money, and the countryside remains peaceful.

Clearly the Peace Corps and the Air Commandos are engaged in the same enterprise. They are preventing violent
unrest in the interests of the United States and secondarily,
the host government. The military does not work in the universities, and the Peace Corps does not work with the native
army, but in the countryside they do the same work. In

Thailand the commandos work in the more dangerous areas, and the Peace Corps takes preventive action where insurgency has not yet appeared.

In a sense the Peace Corps is the advance guard of the military, for it can go into countries where there is not yet an American military presence and do the work which may make a military involvement unnecessary. And if rebellion breaks out while it is there, as occurred in the Dominican Republic, then the Marines can be brought in to put it down, after which, the Peace Corps can return to the work of pacification.

Medical care for the suffering and education for the ignorant are good things whether they are provided by the Peace Corps or the Air Force Commandos. By my values the carrot is better than the stick, and if we are forced to make distinctions, I suppose that bribery is better than napalm. But for a student of international relations, other issues are also of concern. What sort of world are the Peace Corps and the Air Commandos working together to build? The signs seem to me clearly to point to a vast empire of the rich centered in North America, served by poor people all over the world who are kept from rebellion by subtle pacifiers masquerading as agents of change. It is a world in which, metaphorically speaking, the poor will be taught to raise chickens so that the rich can eat fresh eggs.

VII: COLONIES AND SEMI-COLONIES

"In all the forms of government and administrative provisions which they are authorized to prescribe, the commission should bear in mind that the government which they are establishing is designed not for our satisfaction, or for the expression of our theoretical views, but for the happiness, peace, and prosperity of the people of the Philippine Islands, and the measures adopted should be made to conform to their customs, their habits, and even their prejudices, to the fullest extent consistent with the accomplishment of the indispensable requisites of just and effective government.

"At the same time the commission should bear in mind, and the people of the islands should be made plainly to understand, that there are certain great principles of government which have been made the basis of our governmental system which we deem essential to the rule of law and the maintenance of individual freedom, and of which they have, unfortunately, been denied the experience possessed by us: that there are also certain practical rules of government which we have found to be essential to the preservation of these great principles of liberty and law, and that these principles and these rules of government must be established and maintained in their islands for the sake of their liberty and happiness, however, much they may conflict with the customs or laws of procedure with which they are familiar. . . ."

President McKinley to Commissioners of the Philippines on organizing the new civil government, April 7, 1900.

Bikini is a tropical island made famous as the name of a bathing suit, but only a few have ever heard of Elugelab and Rongelap. In the case of Elugelab, it probably doesn't make any difference, for this little island no longer exists. It was vaporized by the explosion of man's first thermonuclear device on November 1, 1952. All that remains is a cavity on the ocean floor.

Rongelap still exists however. On March 1, 1954 the United States government exploded its first deliverable H-bomb at Bikini. It was designed to have a force of about ten megatons. Instead, it turned out to be fifteen. Unexpectedly, it deposited fallout over an area of more than 7,000 square miles, including Rongelap, 105 nautical miles from the detonation. The people of Rongelap received an estimated dose of 175r whole body radiation, and within 24 to 48 hours were experiencing anorexia, nausea, vomiting, and diarrhea.[1]

The people of Rongelap were moved to another island by the U.S. government, but were allowed to return home in June of 1957 after the radiation levels on their island were declared low enough for safety. They were visited for a half day in 1961 by a mission from the United Nations. Many complained to the mission of poor health and deformed children. They said that some fish and some roots which they used to eat now caused boils in their mouths. The Atomic Energy Commission, however, said that the island was free of radiation, and the U.S. administering authorities told the U.N. mission that the problems were "more psychological than real." "Regardless of the view taken by the Administering Authority of the general health situation," declared the U.N. mission in its official report, "the malaise of the Rongelap community is a disturbing fact and the Mission thinks that the Administering Authority should take active steps to rehabilitate the community. As part of such a program, the Mission feels that it might help to restore the confidence of the people if responsible officials of the Administration were to live among them for a period, sharing their food and their anxieties and assisting them in the process of rehabilitation."[2]

In the summer of 1968 it was revealed that the complaints of the people of Rongelap were, contrary to the opinion of the U.S. authorities, more real than psychological. A medical team from the Brookhaven National Laboratory reported that all but two of the nineteen Rongelap children who were less than ten years old at the time of the Bikini detonation had developed abnormal thyroid glands. Nine of them had been treated surgically, and three more and an adult were brought to the U.S. for study. All were being treated with a thyroid extract to prevent further stunting of growth.[3] It is obvious, even to laymen, that the full effects of the radiation on the islanders cannot be assessed for some time to come.

The 1961 United Nations Visiting Mission to the Trust Territories of the Pacific Islands was the first to deal exclusively with these United States controlled islands. Previous missions had dealt with all four Pacific trust territories, and had, therefore, given the American holdings less detailed attention. From 1961 the U.N. began looking more carefully at what the United States was doing, and the resulting reports became an increasing source of embarrassment to Washington.

The Trust Territories of the Pacific Islands, more frequently called Micronesia, consist of 2,100 islands scattered in three million square miles of ocean extending 2,700 miles from west to east and 1,300 miles from north to south. If all of the islands were combined into one land mass it would have an area of only 700 square miles. That is less than Western Samoa (1,130) and Fiji (7,055). The total population is about 97,000 people, and they live on about 100 of the islands. The overall population growth rate is 4% annually which, if it continues, will increase the population to 110,000 by 1971. Only two islands, Saipan and Koror, have more than 4,000 people, and there are ten major linguistic groups. The Trust Territory, therefore, is enormously spread out, unconnected, and difficult to organize into a single, cohesive political unit.

The first European power to establish extensive holdings in Micronesia was Spain. After the Spanish-American war of 1898, Spain lost some of the islands to the United States, and sold others to Germany. After World War I, Japan took over the German holdings as a League of Nations mandate, and most of Micronesia came under Japanese control. It was from the great naval bases in the islands, developed after Japan quit the League, that the Japanese attacked Pearl Harbor, conquered the Solomons, and mounted the offensive toward Australia. During World War II Micronesia became the scene of bloody combat as one by one, at terrible cost, American fighting men captured the main islands in preparation for the assault on the Japanese homeland. Some 3,400 American soldiers and marines died taking Saipan. It is now a major U.S. military base and the seat of the government of the Trust Territory.

After the war, the United States acquired a United Nations trusteeship over Micronesia which permitted the fortification of the islands, but obligated the United States, under U.N. supervision, to provide for the welfare of the native inhabitants. Since then, U.S. policy has been determined primarily by strategic considerations. The islands provide good naval and air bases, and a testing ground for the development of nuclear weapons and delivery systems. Administration was at first divided between the Departments of the Navy and Interior. The military had a lot of money to spend, and did a considerable amount of development work. The Interior budget was small. The result was that outside of military needs, the islands were neglected. Whereas the Japanese had built many roads, factories, and utilities, the United States did virtually nothing. That which the Japanese had built, and which had survived American bombardment, was allowed to deteriorate. Roads were reclaimed by the jungle, and factories were left to stand idle. Under American trusteeship, Micronesia became a vast oceanic Watts, partially radioactive.

It is fortunate for the United States that the Visiting Missions from the United Nations never had members who were really anti-American. The reports of the triennial visits always included much praise of the few things that the United States was doing, and the criticism was always couched in moderate language. But even with their great consideration for American sensibilities, the successive reports of the U.N. missions present a rather ugly picture, one which Soviet representatives to the Trusteeship Council were able to use effectively for propaganda purposes. In 1961 the mission said that "the economy had been allowed to remain static for too long." In 1964 it said that "the results of the so-called realistic financial policy became plain to see not only in the run-down state of many roads, inadequate houses and shabby buildings over considerable parts of the territory, but equally in the stagnant economy and the growing impatience among those quite numerous Micronesians who were aware of other standards." [4] The 1967 mission found again that "the economy is virtually stagnant."

President Kennedy was greatly troubled by the 1961 U.N. report, and appointed an inter-departmental commission to inquire into the future of the Trust Territory. In 1962 the administrative role of the Navy department was ended, and the entire territory was placed under the Department of the Interior. The congressional appropriation for administration and welfare services had been slightly more than $6-million annually. In fiscal year 1963 it was raised to $15-million, and in 1968 is was $24-million. But these are small amounts compared with the need.

The greatest embarrassment to the United States came in 1965 when Dr. Arobati Hicking and ten other members of the professional staff of the Department of Medical Services in Micronesia submitted a petition to U.N. Secretary General U Thant. It was a powerful indictment of the state of health facilities and services in the islands. Hospital equipment, said the petition, "for the most part is ancient, decrepit, or non-existent." "It is impossible with the equipment available to take a useful chest x-ray in most of the Territory . . . Many mental patients are confined in jail or cages because psychiatric facilities are nonexistent." [5]

The petition was forwarded by U Thant to the Trusteeship Council which dispatched a special investigating team of medical professionals from the World Health Organization to investigate the complaints of the petitioners. The team was in the islands for over a month beginning in October, 1965. Its published report confirmed most of the allegations in the petition, although it said some were overstated. While the team was in the islands, there was an outbreak of enteritis, but on one island the responsible agent could not even be identified because there were no microbiological facilities. "A program for long-term, systematic tuberculosis control in the whole territory and instructions for carrying out such a program do not exist," said the report. "The existing laboratory facilities are not sufficient for the proper diagnosis and treatment of tuberculosis . . . Gastroenteritis is common throughout the Territory and is a major cause of child mortality . . . Amoebiasis is very common. Ascoriasis is said to affect 90 per cent of the population . . ." [6] The team found that piped water was available to only a few, and that water treatment was not fully adequate. There were poor garbage facilities, and inadequate toilets in the schools. There was some modern hospital equipment, but much was decrepit as the petitioners had said.

Everywhere there was a shortage of adequately trained personnel, and in the entire Territory there were only five nurses whose qualifications would entitle them to registration in the United States. There was one nurse per 18,000 people compared to three per thousand in the United States. The budget for a single U.S. naval hospital on Guam was $2-million, but the total health budget for the entire Trust Territory was only $1.9-million. Since the standard of comparison used by the investigating team was a statement by President Kennedy that "health services in the Trust Territory shall be at least to the minimum acceptable standards of the United States Community," it was all very embarrassing. "The status of public health services in the Trust Territory of the Pacific Islands," the report concluded, "as found by the team, was still below the standards that the Administration has set itself . . . There was, therefore, justification for the complaints in the petition and the team cannot but agree that certain statements in the health section of the sixteenth annual report of the Administering Authority [the U.S. government] to the United Nations on the Trust Territory of the Pacific Islands were inaccurate and others were liable to create misleading impressions." [7]

As with other U.N. reports there were compliments for things that were done well, for plans and for future intentions, and the whole report was couched in the most moderate diplomatic language. But it was, on balance, a rather damaging exposé of a policy of neglect.

In early 1968 a U.S. Congressional delegation visited Micronesia and saw some of the conditions that had impressed the United Nations. Representative Patsy Mink of Hawaii told how there was no running water on the first day of her visit to Majuro, the District Center for the Marshall Islands. In notes she later read into the *Congressional Record,* she said:

"We had water on the second day only because it rained! Most of the island is entirely without any running water at all — only what can be saved — caught off the rusted iron roofs into gasoline drums that are old, slimy and rusted. Of course, most of the natives have no electricity . . . They live almost exclusively on fish and coconut, and in season, breadfruit and pandanus. Much of the fish is poisonous in the area and many natives still die from eating them. Amoebic dysentery is rampant and nearly no vegetable crops of any kind will grow on the rocky coral ground . . .

"No American community no matter how poor could tolerate the conditions under which these people live . . .

"I heard a doctor tell me that over 80% of the children are infested with roundworms and then go on to say that 'It's okay—They seem to do well with them' — besides even if you did get rid of the worms in a child he would be infested again because he lives without water, without toilets, without refrigeration for food, without screens to keep out the flies, etc." [8]

It has become increasingly apparent since 1961 that the U.N. supervision of the Micronesian trusteeship would be a source of mounting embarrassment for the United States, particularly in the developing world. Not only do the U.N. reports receive world wide publicity, but the Micronesians have discovered that the U.N. provides an excellent vehicle for them to put pressure on the United States. There has been at least one demonstration in the islands, and Micronesians have lobbied delegates at the United Nations.

As yet, however, there is nothing that could be called a nationalist or independence movement in Micronesia. There are several reasons for this. The vast distance between islands, the poor communications, the differences in language, and the absence of group consciousness have made political organization on a territorial basis extremely difficult. But there has been discontent, particularly on those islands that once witnessed Japanese economic development activities. The roads, the factories and the consumer goods are remembered, and the islanders want them back. While the people are not yet trained to function in the modern twentieth century world, neither are they able to return to the simple life

made famous for other parts of the Pacific by Paul Gauguin
and Robert Louis Stevenson. Pressure to move forward is
building.

But what does forward mean? There is hardly any senti-
ment for sovereign independence, for those islanders who
think about such matters believe that they are too weak economically for that, and too vulnerable strategically. Some
want affiliation with the United States. There is strong senti-
ment on Saipan for separation from the Trust Territory and
annexation to the U.S. Territory of Guam. This is because
Chamorro is the language of both Saipan and Guam, and
much of the Saipan economy is now controlled by Guam
businessmen. Elsewhere people talk of commonwealth status
like that of Puerto Rico, but in general there has not been
a very imaginative discussion of the range of possible alter-
natives, and there is certainly no consensus among the islanders.

The plan of the Johnson administration was to hold a
plebiscite in 1972. It is unlikely that before that time there
would develop any effective nationalist movement and hence
there would be no demand for total independence. Meanwhile, the Trust Administration could prepare public opinion
to vote for the specific arrangement most desired by Washington. Whether or not such a scheme has yet been designed,
it is safe to predict that it will be one that will get the United
Nations and its embarrassing reports off of Washington's
back.

It is in this context that the decision was made to send the
Peace Corps into Micronesia. As Director Jack Vaughn told
the Senate Foreign Relations Committee in 1967: "Last year
we were approached by [United Nations] Ambassador Goldberg and Secretary [of the Interior] Udall with regard to a
problem that had been reported by a number of sources —
the United Nations, our Ambassador [to the Trusteeship

Council] Eugenie Anderson — on the slowness of economic and social development in Micronesia . . . And the Micronesians themselves were unhappy at the slow rate of progress . . ." [9]

Clearly the Peace Corps was being called to bail the United States out of a political problem in the United Nations, and it was a brilliant idea. First of all, it was a cheap solution, infinitely less expensive than providing the professional manpower that the islands needed. Second, the volunteers are conditioned to make do with what is available, not to make demands for money to buy supplies and equipment. Third, the volunteers would live with the local population, eat their food and share in the native life. In doing this they would have a much greater influence than professionals who would live in big houses and socialize only with other Americans.[10] Fourth, the volunteers would be dedicated, hard working, idealistic young people, who, by their very presence, would communicate the notion that the people of the United States really care about the Micronesians. And finally, after two years of service in Micronesia, the volunteers would constitute a trained manpower pool from which to recruit future administrators and teachers.

Given the inexperience and lack of independence of the newly created Micronesian legislature (over which the High Commission has a veto), it was not difficult to elicit from it a request for Peace Corps Volunteers. Shortly after this was received in April, 1966, President Johnson called for "the greatest possible involvement on the part of the Peace Corps." What followed was a crash program of considerable size. By the end of 1966 the Peace Corps had recruited, trained, and deployed in Micronesia 460 Volunteers. As of September 30, 1968 another 550 were in training. The sixth annual report (1968) claimed a ratio of one Volunteer for every 300 Micronesians, "the highest distribution rate of any program in the agency's history."

Most of the Volunteers in Micronesia are working as teachers, and the teaching of English is their main subject. They apparently impressed the 1967 U.N. Visiting Mission more with their dedication than their professionalism. "The Mission was impressed," said their report, "by the keenness of the Volunteers but had reservations about the wisdom of sending to the Territory persons who were not qualified teachers even though they had received some instruction in the teaching of English as a second language." [11]

This is a little unrealistic. Of course, professional, more experienced teachers would be better, but quite clearly the United States does not care enough about the Micronesians to pay the costs. Moreover, it is possible that Peace Corps teachers who live with the local population may be able to produce results faster than professional teachers who would probably remain aloof. In 1968, one Volunteer, Catherine Dancy, was even teaching on Rongelap, where professionals might be unwilling to go. The Peace Corps estimates that 70 to 75 per cent of the total Micronesian student population is being taught by Volunteers, and it points with pride to the results of a standard achievement test administered in the Marianas which showed a "phenomenal" 8.5 month growth in average student achievement "directly attributable to the input of 22 Volunteer teachers." [12] Clearly the Peace Corps contribution to Micronesian education is an enormous improvement over anything that existed previously.

The emphasis on English teaching has profound political implications, for if the Micronesians do learn the language it will inevitably orient them toward the United States, its literature, its technology, its radio and television, its advertising, and its economy. Given the absence of a highly developed culture, as there was, for example, in India when the British arrived, the American culture will find little resistance once the language is established.

Is the Peace Corps, then, helping to impose an Americanization on the Micronesians? It is a question which obviously bothers the Corps administration. "Why should Micronesian students learn English?", asks the training manual for the seventh team of Micronesia-bound Volunteers. "Are we engaging in some sort of covert cultural imperialism, imposing our language power on the Micronesian children? We feel that this is certainly not what we are doing . . . Micronesia's needs in this time of abrupt confrontation with the rest of the world — its politics, its technology — are not the same as they were 100 or even 20 years ago . . . In some respects their languages can no longer serve them adequately. While Trukese, Kusiean, or any of the other Micronesian languages are totally suited to, and are manifestations of *traditional* Micronesian culture, the contemporary Micronesian requires, in addition, a tool which he can use when he is dealing with *untraditional* situations. It is today fully as important for the Micronesian to be able to fix an outboard motor or write a proposal for Grant-in-Aid as it for him to know the secrets of navigation or of breadfruit cultivation. In short, the Micronesian needs a second language as a tool to use in certain areas in which his first language is inadequate. History has dictated that the second language of Micronesia be English." [13]

The argument is quite sound. The twentieth century is invading Micronesia, and cannot be held back so long as Micronesians want medical care and the fruits of industrialism. To survive in the twentieth century they need knowledge they cannot get through the medium of their own language. Conquest has put the United States in control, and the Americans could hardly be expected to teach Spanish or Japanese. Clearly, English is the language the Micronesians must be taught.

At the same time it is important to recognize what this

means. It *is* cultural imperialism of the same kind that Macaulay pursued in India, and it has certain far-reaching consequences. For the Peace Corps not to admit this and discuss it is dishonest and short-sighted, although it may be politically impossible for it to do otherwise.

For a considerable time, until all Micronesians become fluent in English, they will be at a disadvantage in their relationships with Americans, and the best that they can hope for is a benevolent paternalism. This situation will last as long as the Americans are able to keep their paternalism subtle and inoffensive, which the Peace Corps is adept at doing. Its duration will also depend upon the access to economic and political power allowed to ambitious, and talented Micronesians. It was the inadequacy of such access that produced the nationalist movement in India which ultimately expelled the British. But it must also be remembered that the Indian nationalist movement would have been impossible without the English language that enabled Indians of different regions to unite in a common organization, the Indian National Congress. And it should also be noted that the Congress was founded by a Macaulay type Englishman, Alan Octavian Hume, a retired civil servant.

While the teaching of English may, in the short run, strengthen dependency, it may, if done well, lay the foundation for greater independence in the long run. With English, Micronesians may learn to do for themselves what, without it, they would always have to depend on foreigners to do for them. But whether the teaching of English is a contribution to nation-building, as the Peace Corps asserts, or the beginning of assimilation, cannot yet be determined. Here again the experience of India may be instructive, for there are signs that despite Indian nationalism, despite the post-independence revolt against English and the return to the technologically inadequate regional vernaculars, the Indian government is finding itself increasingly dependent upon Britain's successor, the United States, for military and economic assistance. This is symbolized by the massiveness of the Peace Corps program in India, escalated suddenly after Prime Minister Gandhi's visit to Washington in 1966. As of September 1968, 2,122 Volunteers had served or were serving in India. It was by far the largest Peace Corps program in the entire world. It was concentrated on food production rather than education, but it was able to function only because of the English language.

Although the main Peace Corps effort in Micronesia is in education, Volunteers are working in other areas as well, especially health and agriculture. In general, Volunteer deployment is determined by Trust Administration policy. "There are no Peace Corps programs in Micronesia," says a Peace Corps briefing paper. "There are Trust Territory programs for which the Peace Corps provides manpower. This is an important distinction as the Peace Corps does not wish to be viewed as an agency independent of the administration. We work with and for the Trust Territory Government." [14]

One of the most interesting areas is in the field of law. On Ponape, one Volunteer helped set up the Peace Corps Legal Services with an office located in the District Court House. The purpose of the organization is to provide advice to Micronesian lawyers, not to take on cases. The lawyer Volunteer also serves as legislative council for the fledgling district legislature, helping the legislators draft bills and redraft measures that are vetoed on legal technicalities. He has also advised the court, assisted the public defender, helped start a legal journal, helped start a newspaper, advised the high school debate team, and worked on assorted other projects. Clearly the influence of this one Volunteer in shaping the direction of the Micronesian polity has been

rather extensive. At the same time it has been done in such
a way as to encourage Micronesians to help themselves, not
to turn their problems over to Americans. The Peace Corps
appears to take seriously the idea that it is preparing the
Micronesians for "self-determination", although it is never
very precise about what that means. Yet obviously what the
Peace Corps is doing is constructing a firm basis for a
permanent relationship with the United States.

Whether this is good or bad depends upon one's values,
one's political theories, and one's view of the imperatives of
world politics. My own opinion is that the Micronesians are
being prepared for a political arrangement that will keep
them under United States control, but deprive them of any
real power to affect their collective destinies. Once annexed,
they will be treated like the American Indians on their reservations, which is to say not very well. The best way for them
to avoid this, it seems to me, is to preserve some relationship
with the United Nations, for only under the prodding of the
Russians and others is the United States likely to give the
islands the help they need.

Another factor that should also be kept in mind when
evaluating the role of the Peace Corps in Micronesia is that
the primary interest of the United States there is strategic.
We want to use the islands as bases, and as testing grounds
for missiles. Kwajalein, for example, is our main proving
ground for testing anti-ballistic-missile missiles. Should re-
surgent Japanese nationalism force us to give up our bases
in Japan and Okinawa, the trust islands will assume even
greater importance as strategic bases. For the United States,
Micronesia is essentially a military enterprise, and the work
of the Peace Corps serves primarily to obscure and falsely
legitimize this fact.

While Micronesia is not technically a colony of the United
States, the relationship is quite clearly colonial in character,

and the Volunteer there is simply a new form of underpaid colonial civil servant. It is important to remember this because it makes it easier to understand the world-wide function of the Peace Corps. It is my contention that its role everywhere is essentially the same, differing only in detail. The difference is determined primarily by the extent to which sovereignty rests with native decision makers. Thus in the countries which are dependencies of the United States, its role is to strengthen the economic, cultural, and political ties with America. The long range effect is to purloin sovereignty by increasing the influence of Washington. In countries which are less dependent upon the United States, the Volunteers prepare public opinion for American penetration by projecting an appealing image and by helping to create desires that require a certain "Americanization" to satisfy.

The colonial civil servant aspect of Peace Corps service can be seen also in the high concentration of Volunteers in Liberia. Liberia's relationship to the United States differs from that of Micronesia's more in degree than in kind. Liberia is legally a sovereign state, but its economy is controlled by Americans, and American currency is the country's only legal tender. Liberia has permitted the construction and operation from Liberian soil of one of the largest transmitters of the Voice of America. It enables the United States to broadcast to all of Africa. Also located in Liberia is Roberts Field, a major United States base during World War II and a potential springboard for American military operations in West Africa.

The grip of American interests on the Liberian economy can be seen clearly in the field of banking. The Bank of Monrovia, which is the government bank and the bank of issue, is owned 100% by the International Banking Corporation, which in turn is owned by the First National City Bank of New York. 49% of the Bank of Liberia is owned by the Chemical Bank of New York. The Liberian Trade and Development Bank is 50% owned by the Bankers Trust Company of New York; the other 50% is owned by the Banco di Credito Finanziario of Milan. Chase Manhattan also has a Liberian branch, and Americans own the International Trust Company of Liberia.[15]

President William V. S. Tubman's "Open Door" policy makes investment attractive for American investors. Corporate law is based on U.S. statutes, books and records may be kept in a firm's home office, and funds may be banked in any country. Labor is cheap. In 1964 wages averaged fifteen cents an hour for industrial workers and eight cents an hour for agricultural workers. The Firestone Rubber Company, the biggest and most influential firm in Liberia, paid latex tappers 64 cents a day. Anthropologists and Peace Corps Volunteers report that Firestone also uses corvée labor.[16] In 1966, 10,000 Firestone tappers struck but were severely put down by troops after President Tubman declared the strike "illegal." The moderately conservative American journal, *Africa Report,* commented that "the government's draconian controls appear to exceed the need." [17]

Liberia also has rich iron ore deposits which are being exploited by Americans. The largest mining enterprise in Liberia is the Liberian American Swedish Minerals Company (LAMCO) which has a concession of 500 square miles. LAMCO was set up with $60-million from Bethlehem Steel, $55-60 million from an African, American, and Swedish syndicate, $30-million from the U.S. Export-Import Bank, and $5.7-million from the First National City Bank. The other big mining company is the Liberia Mining Company owned 60% by Republic Steel.[18] Foreign concessionaires of one kind or another create about one-half of Liberia's gross domestic product.

Since its beginning Liberia has been dominated by the Americo-Liberian descendents of the freed American slaves who founded the country under American tutelage. It is governed by an oligarchy based on kinship with the dictatorial President Tubman.[19] The oligarchy is the fulcrum of the alliance between the foreign concessionaires and the coast-dwelling Americo-Liberians. This power bloc drains away the wealth needed to raise the standard of living of the inland tribes which constitute 90% of Liberia's total population. Some flavor of the evils of such an arrangement can be found in Fletcher Knebel's novel about the Peace Corps, The *Zin-Zin Road.*[20] Written after Knebel visited Liberia on assignment from the Peace Corps, it deals with the mythical country Kalya which is quite similar to Liberia, although it bears some resemblance to Malawi as well.

It is unlikely that the impoverished condition of the tribal people of Liberia can be substantially alleviated without breaking the hold of Tubman and the Americo-Liberians. At the same time it is difficult to imagine the emergence of an effective revolutionary government even if Tubman were overthrown. Ignorance, tribal differences, superstition, and lack of experience in modern statecraft cannot form the basis of good government, yet these are the outstanding characteristics of the Liberian polity today. While a revolution may be necessary, the revolutionaries would have a difficult time effecting change, certainly more difficult than that experienced by Fidel Castro in Cuba, for example.

On the other hand, the reinforcement of the existing oligarchy is also unlikely to facilitate change. While its power remains intact, the best that can be hoped for is that modernization of the economy by foreign investors will produce more jobs and some income improvement at the lower levels. Corruption can be alleviated by the introduction of modern management techniques and the infusion of foreign personnel into the bureaucracy. The Peace Corps is facilitating this process by means of its program in public administration. Meanwhile, despite the personal hostility of many Volunteers to the ruling oligarchy, the educational and health work they do in the countryside helps to create the impression that the government cares about the people and that there is movement in the right direction. Above all, the Peace Corps projects an image of Americans as dedicated, altruistic, and incorruptible, and thereby prepares the ground for public acceptance of a greater assumption by them of decision-making power.

With respect to real, *de facto* sovereignty, the differences between Liberia and Micronesia are not great. Each is dominated by the United States; neither can plan a future which does not enjoy United States approval. Both are placated by the Peace Corps.

As the United States continues to expand, it is not hard to imagine how more and more countries may be brought into a similar relationship. Ethiopia is a likely prospect, where English has been made the medium of instruction in the schools and where some Peace Corps officials speak with pride of the virtual takeover by Volunteers of the school system.

The Peace Corps program began in Ethiopia in May of 1962 when the Ethiopian Ministry of Education requested 300 volunteers. By September of that year, 277 were at work in Ethiopian schools. As of February, 1968, more than 1,100 Volunteers had served or were serving as teachers in the school system, and the 350 volunteers teaching at that moment made up a third of all secondary school teachers and nearly half of the core curriculum teachers. As of July 31, 1968, a total of 1,507 Volunteers had served in the country.[21] "In 1967," says an official Peace Corps description of the program in Ethiopia, "Volunteers were teaching in 96 schools located in 79 communities. They currently are teaching in all government secondary schools, and 45 percent of the government junior-secondary schools. Perhaps most significantly, nearly all of the Ethiopian secondary graduates who entered seventh grade in or after 1964 were exposed to a minimum of one Peace Corps Volunteer teacher. . . . Since English is the second official language of Ethiopia, and the language of instruction from the seventh grade on, the contribution of Peace Corps English teachers cannot be overestimated." [22]

As of February, 1968, there were 26 Volunteers teaching at the Haile Selassie University, and there were 17 Volunteers assigned to the four Teacher Training Institutes where the Peace Corps would influence the Ethiopian teachers who would go out into the rural schools.

As in Micronesia and Liberia, the Peace Corps is also interested in the legal structure of Ethiopia. At least 22 Volunteer lawyers have served in Ethiopia in a variety of assignments. Some worked with the Institute of Public Administration on the consolidation of Ethiopian law, a task reminiscent of that undertaken by Macaulay in India. (See Chapter III, pp. 29-31). "The objective of the Lawyer Program," says the Peace Corps, "is to provide desperately needed professional skill to the IEG [Imperial Ethiopian Government] at a time when legislative and constitutional changes are being made which will affect Ethiopia for many years to come. The contribution of the PCV lawyer is to improve the quality of legislation that is passed, the procedures that are adopted, and the actions that are taken. They are also involved in training in the sense that almost every Ministry employee they work with is exposed to their approach to solving problems, and to their insistence on

rational argument, careful preparation and complete docu-
mentation." [23]

One Peace Corps Volunteer lawyer functioned as a broker
between the Ethiopian Ministry of Public Works and USAID.
According to the Peace Corps he "saved" an urban housing
program that was being underwritten by AID by showing the
Ministry how to conform to AID requirements. One PCV lawyer worked at drafting land reform legislation, another
helped establish a legal department for the Imperial Board
of Telecommunications, and still another prepared the brief
which helped his IEG agency win a dispute with a U.S. con-
tractor.

It is impossible to evaluate the impact of all of these projects on the political economy of Ethiopia. A great deal depends upon how well each individual task is done and what
sort of impression it makes on those who hold, or will in the
future hold, power in Ethiopia. During the early period the
Peace Corps did not make a good impression. At one time
secondary students went on strike against Peace Corps teachers, because they felt the Volunteers' innovative methods did
not prepare them for the national examinations. According
to David E. Berlew, the Peace Corps Director in Ethiopia,
"we came to realize that despite our claims to the contrary,
we were in fact trying to make Ethiopians over in our own
image and becoming discouraged and disillusioned when
they did not respond." Berlew went on to say that in Ethiopia,
as in most countries, "you have to be able to function effectively within the system if you want to influence it," that the
Peace Corps had learned this, and that "whereas two years
ago the government was requesting fewer and fewer Volunteers, the trend has reversed and now we are not able to
meet its requests. Their new confidence in us has opened
many doors that have hitherto been closed to us . . ." [24] The

expansion of Peace Corps influence in Africa, as everywhere, depends upon subtlety.

Whatever its skill and competence, it is clear that the Peace Corps has penetrated the most strategic institutions of Ethiopian society, and is in a position to exert a considerable influence on the long range development of the country. The protracted exposure of existing and potential elites to Volunteers makes Ethiopia more susceptible to the development of a relationship similar to that between the U.S. and Liberia. An awareness of this may be developing among Ethiopian youth. On March 28, 1969, a group of about fifty Ethiopian students invaded the Ethiopian chancery building in Washington protesting "a social system rendered obsolete by history." They charged that "the U.S. supported feudal regime in Ethiopia has recently intensified its brutal oppression of the Ethiopian masses." According to their leader, Esana Tatek, the students were demanding the repeal of new educational fees, the resignation of the minister of education and the removal from Ethiopia of the Peace Corps.[25]

I believe that it is instructive to locate Micronesia, Liberia, and Ethiopia at one end of a spectrum of relationships resulting from American expansionism. Micronesia, of course, is the extreme case, a virtual colony with the role of viceroy played by the High Commissioner. Only world public opinion, mobilized through the United Nations, limits the sovereignty of the United States over the Micronesians. Liberia has greater flexibility and less formalized American dominance. Moreover, American dominance there is pluralistic, not concentrated in an agency of government, but distributed among U.S. government agencies and private financial interests. Ethiopia has even greater independence, although the foundation of increased American domination is being carefully, if not altogether deliberately, constructed. After the assumption of the Peace Corps directorship by Jack Vaughn, the Peace Corps began moving into more countries of the Ethiopian type, countries that are less noted for democratic government than for personalized rule and sympathy for American interests. Among the new additions are South Korea, Guyana (under Burnham, not Jagan), Paraguay, and Nicaragua.

Whereas in Micronesia Peace Corps Volunteers are simply colonial civil servants, in these other countries they are the advance men of American expansionism. Like Boy Scouts, they do some good deeds, and they make a good impression. They also learn the languages and cultures, so that in the future they may either become a manpower pool for governmental tasks, or they may go into the domestic United States educational system and help prepare a new generation of young idealists to go abroad to safeguard America's interests.

VIII: THE UNSUITABLES

Rep. Myers: "I think what we are talking about is the type of people we have serving in the Peace Corps."

Rep. Gallagher: "My friend, if you are going to question the type of people who are serving in the Peace Corps, I do not think you can find anyone more dedicated than those kids."

Rep. Myers: ". . . I think everyone in this chamber should seriously question if a young man would rather give up his citizenship in this great country than serve in the Armed Forces, whether that man should be serving in the Peace Corps."

Rep. Gallagher: "Mr. Chairman, no one challenges that."

Rep. Morgan: "Mr. Chairman, if the gentlemen furnishes the names, I will do my best to bring every one of those people home from the Peace Corps. I assure the gentleman that I will be in direct contact with the Director of the Peace Corps and see if we cannot get those individuals out of the Peace Corps."

Excerpts from debate in the House of Representatives, June 13, 1968.

Most of the people who volunteer for the Peace Corps are unsuitable from the Corps' point of view, and are never invited to join. Their application blanks or their letters of recommendation provide evidence that they are not good material. Others pass the initial hurdle, but exhibit disqualifying features in training. It is the task of the Office of Selection to detect and encourage them to resign. But some get through training and are assigned to posts overseas before their unsuitability is discovered. They become "early terminations"—that is, they are sent home.

Early terminations result from a variety of difficulties. Most of them have to do with "personal adjustment", a category that covers everything from psychic disturbances to just plain goofing off. It includes early terminations due to "indiscreet" behavior relating to sex and drugs, which, in the opinion of the Peace Corps, might discredit the organization's reputation and thus reduce its effectiveness. One such case

117

was Alan Weiss who has written of his training experiences in a book entitled *High Risk/High Gain.* Weiss says that when his girl friend came from the states to be with him in Nigeria he was told he was in violation of regulations against importing women from abroad. He was asked to resign, and did.

In general the Peace Corps takes a tolerant view of sexual freedom and asks only that the Volunteers be discreet and not embarrass the Corps. Given the extreme differences in sex mores among the cultures in which the Corps functions, it sometimes becomes a difficult matter to decide what is indiscreet. For example, what is the proper response for a male Volunteer whom a tribal chief wishes to honor by sending one of his wives to spend the night? Volunteers who have served in Africa report that when they engage in sexual practices that are perfectly acceptable in local cultures it produces an irrational, "uptight" reaction among U.S. embassy and AID personnel. While the sex issue has created some problems from time to time, Volunteers in general do not appear to behave differently than other Americans, and most of them exercise better judgment or more discretion than Alan Weiss.

Although the Peace Corps seems to have adjusted to sex it is still having trouble with drugs. Evidence of increased usage of marijuana among potential Volunteers has made it difficult for the Corps to set policy that will not seriously impair recruitment. Some indication of the rapidly escalating nature of the problem can be seen in the proliferation of policy directives. Selection Policy Notice No. 109 on drug usage issued on August 2, 1968, had to be revised the following month. "Without exception," said the September 13 revision, "no one for whom we have evidence of marijuana or hallucinogens use WILL GO OVERSEAS OR BE SWORN IN AS A VOLUNTEER WITHOUT AN APPROVAL FROM PEACE CORPS WASH-

INGTON." The directive said that "any use of marijuana or hallucinogens during Peace Corps service, including service as a trainee, is grounds for termination."

There is not much public data on drug user terminations. Returned Volunteers have told me that marijuana is easily available in some countries and fairly widely used by PCV's. In India, the forum of elected Volunteer delegates held in New Delhi in December, 1967, passed a resolution which endorsed the policy of termination for marijuana use, but added: "Recognizing the difficulties of enforcing this policy, we have confidence the Regional Directors will enforce this policy in a rational manner." [1] It is obvious that as long as marijuana is both illegal and popular with adventurous young people, the Peace Corps will have a serious problem on its hands.

While they may be less numerous than terminations that result from personal adjustment reasons, it is the political terminations that attract the most attention and have the greatest impact on the character of the Peace Corps. Two cases have become international *causes celebres*. The first was the famous case of Margery Michelmore whose post card describing poverty in Nigeria fell into nationalist hands and became the basis of an anti-American propaganda campaign. Miss Michelmore was not actually terminated, but was brought back to Washington where she worked in the Peace Corps headquarters for a while. The uproar alerted many bureaucrats and Volunteers to the sensitivities of developing nations and to the political importance of the Peace Corps.

The Michelmore case was an accident; the Bruce Murray case was not. Murray was a 25 year-old musician from Newport, Rhode Island, who had an M.A. in musical composition from UCLA. He joined the Peace Corps in 1965. "I felt honestly," he said later, "that I was lucky and had gotten a good education, and in some way this could be of use to somebody in another country." He thought he would be assigned to "digging latrines" or some other unglamorous task, but instead was sent to teach music at the University of Concepcion in Chile.

Murray appears to have been a model Volunteer. Not only did he do his teaching well, but he took on extra tasks in the community. He taught some boys in jail to sing, and he formed three choral groups of young girls. Feeling that the university environment brought him into contact only with the middle and upper classes, he moved into a shanty town on the outskirts of the city. "By living in the poorer section," he said, "I got to know people in the lowest income bracket and it gave me a fuller picture of life in Chile." The young musician liked his life and was thinking of extending his service beyond the normal two year period.

Murray had never exhibited much interest in political matters, and said he "very seldom discussed politics with anyone." In May, 1967, a petition calling for a bombing halt in Vietnam began circulating among Volunteers in Chile. By the end of the month the 13 Volunteers who were circulating the petition had reportedly collected 92 signatures from among the 442 Volunteers serving in Chile.[2] When word of the petition reached U.S. Ambassador Ralph Dungan, he called in the original 13 Volunteers and tried to stop their efforts. "I told them," he explained, "that individual expression is one thing—group actions as volunteers is quite another."

Dungan asked the Volunteers to state their position in a letter to Jack Vaughn, which they did, and on June 7, Vaughn replied. "The Peace Corps," said his letter, "was established as an apolitical organization and it has been our firm belief that preservation of that character is essential to its effectiveness." Vaughn then spelled out policy about the public expression by Volunteers of opinions on politics. "You may," he said, "as individuals, express your opinions to the President, the Congress and the U.S. press if you completely avoid public identification of your Peace Corps connections, or the danger of such identification. The protection of the Peace Corps can be achieved, without any loss in freedom of expression, by making clear in your private communications to the President or members of the Congress that publication of your message would be inconsistent with the apolitical role of the Peace Corps if you were to be identified as a Volunteer or staff member. Letters to the U.S. press for possible publication cannot include your Peace Corps connection or, if a number of you wish to join in a petition, your foreign address, since the latter makes identification almost inevitable. Such messages could be sent to your family or friends for forwarding from United States post offices."

Vaughn's policy, then, not only prohibited Volunteers from identifying themselves, as such, it even said they could not reveal their geographical location lest someone deduce that they were Volunteers. As might be expected, this new edict was deeply resented by the Volunteers in Chile. Bruce Murray, who had signed the original petition, decided to test the policy. He wrote a letter to the *New York Times* protesting both the war in Vietnam and Vaughn's policy. The *Times* did not print the letter but handled the incident as a news story, a wire service version of which was published in Chile. Then Murray translated the letter into Spanish and gave it to the Concepcion paper, *El Sur*, where it was printed.

Vaughn struck back immediately, despite differences of opinion among his top level staff. He recalled Murray and quickly drummed him out of the Corps. The reason for termination was that Murray "had involved himself in a political issue that is contentious in Chile"—that is, the Vietnam war.'

In the letter of dismissal he sent to Murray, Vaughn said: "You have violated Peace Corps policy by having your

opinions on a contentious issue published in a Chilean newspaper. Then you told my staff that, were you to return to
Chile, you would take the issue to the Chilean and United
States press. Your interest is now primarily that of obtain-
ing support for your political views rather than that of service
as a Volunteer. I have no reasonable alternative, therefore,
but to terminate your service with the Peace Corps." [4]

Bruce Murray risked a great deal by fighting Vaughn on
the free speech issue. He had a 2A draft deferment and had
he been allowed to complete his service in Chile, he would
have reached the draft-immune age of twenty-six. However,
as soon as he reached the United States he learned he had
draft problems. "The day I arrived," Murray declared, "I
called home to tell my mother I was back and why, and she
told me she had received a draft reclassification to 1A a few
days prior, and had forwarded it on to me in Chile. Then she
got a call from the clerk of the draft board telling her I was
coming back to the U.S. and to make sure I had the new
draft card. . . . The mystery is how the clerk knew I was
coming back to the U.S. before I had arrived." [5]

When Murray got home to Newport he went to the draft
board and applied for an occupational deferment in order
to return to Chile where the local people had offered him a
job. The board turned him down, and his appeal was rejected. He then applied for classification as a conscientious
objector, but this was also denied. When ordered to appear
for induction he refused, and as of December, 1968, he was
waiting to be tried for violating the selective service laws.
Meanwhile, with the aid of the American Civil Liberties
Union in New York, Murray was bringing suit against the
Peace Corps for having illegally terminated his service and
against his draft board for having acted wrongly in handling
his case.

If Vaughn thought that quick and stern discipline in the

Murray case would quell the revolt, his judgment served him
badly. Murray's dismissal was announced on June 29, 1967.
Ten days later the *New York Times* carried a letter from Paul
Cowan and four other Volunteers in Ecuador protesting both
the war and the new policy on political expression. The war,
said the letter, was "compromising our work as Peace Corps
Volunteers in a direct and personal way." As for the Vaughn
ruling, it "directly contradicts a promise made to us during
our training that the only restriction on our right to write
and speak freely applied to internal politics of the countries
where we were working. Now in effect, we have been ordered
to support the war in Vietnam—with our silence at least—
as long as we remain connected to the Peace Corps."

This, of course, was not strictly accurate. They had not
been ordered to support the war or to remain silent, but
rather to conceal their affiliation with the Peace Corps if they
should express themselves on political matters in public statements. Nevertheless, the effect of the Vaughn directive, if it
had been enforced, would have been to limit, or render less
effective, criticism of the war, and I believe it is fair to say
that a Peace Corps which inhibits criticism of a war is a
Peace Corps that gives aid and comfort to the war makers.
Since Cowan and his colleagues identified themselves as
Volunteers in their letter, they were in clear violation of
Vaughn's new policy. The gauntlet was thrown down.

Within a week of the Ecuador Volunteers' statement, the
New York Times carried another letter on the subject. This
one was by Harris Wofford, formerly Associate Director of
the Peace Corps and now president of the State University
College at Old Westbury, Long Island. Wofford said that
speech restrictions would damage the "magic" of the Peace
Corps, an important part of which was that Volunteers were
"freer agents than ever seen before in any bureaucracy."
"Volunteers," wrote Wofford, "go abroad not as ambassa-

dors, or propaganda agents or civil servants. They go as
citizens—free to agree or disagree with their President, to
agree or disagree with American official policies. . . . They
are making visible what, for too many people around the
world, has usually been invisible about America—our relatively open society." While Volunteers should not interfere
in host country politics, Wofford added, the American public
had a right to know what Volunteers thought about matters
such as the Vietnam war.[6]

In addition to this opposition from Volunteers and from
Wofford, there were critical newspaper editorials and articles,
and the American Civil Liberties Union showed signs of getting involved in the issue. Faced with a major rebellion,
Vaughn backed down. The retreat was described in a carefully phrased article by Stuart Awbrey, the editor of the
Peace Corps Volunteer. The five Ecuador Volunteers had not
been terminated, he declared. "They had not," he wrote,
"injected their views on a contentious political issue into the
host press." Some Volunteers, he pointed out, argued that
Murray had not done so either because the Vietnam war was
not a contentious issue in Chile—everybody was against U.S.
policy. Awbrey continued: "Vaughn followed shortly with
an amendment to the earlier ban on identification with the
Peace Corps in letters home; he said the right to write individual letters to U.S. authorities and journals on U.S. political
issues, using Peace Corps identification or not, was okay
with the Peace Corps."

One implication of this statement is that *group* petitions
of Volunteers as Volunteers were still proscribed. Awbrey
said that the Peace Corps was back where it started, "perched
precariously, as always, on the discretion of its membership."
The controversy, he observed, "has taught the Corps that it
has less to fear from political issues than from restraints on
their discussion."

While the Murray case was more a symptom than a cause of political controversy within the Peace Corps, it does appear to have marked the beginning of some important new activity by Volunteers. Even before Murray wrote his letter there were signs that smoldering Volunteer resentment of the Vietnam war in particular, and U.S. foreign policy in general was beginning to be articulated and organized.

During the same month that the anti-Vietnam petition was circulating in Latin America (May, 1967) the *Peace Corps Volunteer* published a highly personal and revealing article by Paul Cowan in which he described the collapse of his project in Guayaquil and tried to explain why he and other Volunteers had failed. "There was, from the outset," he wrote, "no analysis that connected the kind of 'peaceful revolution' that the Peace Corps dreamed of creating here to the reality that each Volunteer was forced to confront." He said that the work which the Volunteer was trained to do simply did not exist, and that the local officials did not consider the Volunteers very professional.

"Here I feel irrelevant to the society in which I've been placed," Cowan declared. The difference in his standard of living and that of the people he was supposed to help bothered him greatly. "When I stride thorugh the *barrios*, at 6-feet, 2-inches, towering over every Ecuadorian I pass, I feel like a damn colonialist. Can one help it? It's a physical thing. The house I live in, like all Peace Corps houses, is better than anything any of my neighbors will ever be able to afford. I spend more money on food each day than most of my neighbors do in a week. . . . The poor people here, I grow certain, will never be able to enjoy the kind of change I had planned for them. . . . To explain my disappointment I blame the people I work with; to explain theirs they blame me. . . . I find myself wondering whether this horrible poverty is not after all the fault of the poor. . . . Although I write all of this in the first person it rings true, I am sure, for other Volunteers. What ideals are we serving, after all? Whose interests? Here we are in Guayaquil (and in how many other cities of the world?) without much work to do, uncertain that the country wants us, privately cursing the people we came to help."

When Cowan wrote this, there were probably only a few Volunteers in various parts of the world that were entertaining such fundamental doubts about the effect of the Peace Corps. The Bruce Murray case intensified those doubts and increased the number of Volunteers who had them. By the following November, Cowan and his colleagues in Guayaquil had launched a minor revolution. They enlisted the help of the father of a Volunteer who established a mailing address for them in Alexandria, Virginia, and then began circulating a mimeographed manifesto calling for the internationalization of the Peace Corps. The full text was published in the January 17, 1968 issue of *Harvard Crimson* and received considerable attention on other college campuses. "We joined the Peace Corps," said the document, "because we thought it would afford us a means of helping developing nations without imposing the United States' political and cultural values on them. . . . We were wrong. We now see that the Peace Corps is arrogant and colonialist in the same way as the government of which it is a part."

The latent controversies that were brought to the surface by the Bruce Murray case came at the moment when the number of returned Peace Corps Volunteers for the first time outnumbered those currently in service. An official count in the summer of 1967 showed 14,573 returned Volunteers and 14,452 Volunteers in training or overseas.[7] According to the Peace Corps, the United States had become the "number one world-wide recipient of people imbued with the Peace Corps idea." The Corps estimated that nearly two-thirds of the returnees had gone into education, either as teachers or students. Coincidentally, returned Volunteers began to appear on college campuses just at the period when campus opposition to the war in Vietnam and the military-industrial complex began to reach a high intensity. The extent to which the returnees influenced campus activists and vice versa is impossible to say, but I think it is evident that the returnees provided a communications link between the colleges and the Volunteers in the field that intensified discontent with American foreign policy in both places.

During the early years there does not appear to have been much radicalism among the Volunteers, or even much political awareness. This is confirmed by the report of the conference on the returned Peace Corps Volunteer that was held at the State Department in March, 1965. In his summary of the proceedings, Associate Director Harris Wofford reported that as far as political matters went, "it appeared that it was a non-partisan and almost non-political politics that interested them most." In his judgment "Few of the Volunteers seemed inclined to be rebels outside 'the system'." "Most were interested in learning the process of change within the system." [8] Wofford's assessment was echoed by Chris Weeks, the Deputy Director of the Job Corps. "I've seen Peace Corps Volunteers overseas in about six countries," he said, "and the thing that surprised me most today, was the lack of more rebels among the returnees. In our discussion group the primary concern seemed to be, how do I fit back into the system as it is here in the United States. Maybe this is good. But I had expected that we would find more people who might come back here and ask more questions." [9]

There were a few Volunteers at the conference who circulated a petition against the war in Vietnam and considered picketing the White House, but after a talk with Sargent Shriver they decided not to embarrass the Peace Corps.

If Harris Wofford was correct in saying that there was "a non-political tide running among the Volunteers," it probably reached its high mark in that year. The returned Volunteers conference was held just as President Johnson was beginning to escalate the war in Vietnam, and the full impact of the war had not yet been felt either on the Peace Corps or on college campuses. The big demonstrations and draft card burnings were still in the future.

But by 1966 there were already signs of an interest in organizing Volunteers for political purposes. Early that year some returned Volunteers in the New York area began talking of an association of former Volunteers. In December, 1966, an all-day conference was held at Columbia University on "Returnee Influence in Reshaping U.S. Foreign Policy," and out of this meeting came a decision to form a New York area group. Eventually there emerged the Committee of Returned Volunteers (CRV), a loosely organized structure of groups with the strongest contingents in New York, Washington, Boston, Bloomington, and San Francisco.[10]

The Committee of Returned Volunteers stated three goals:
• To remain well-informed about events in developing countries, the course of U.S. policy and involvement;
• To bring CRV concerns regarding policy before the public through the mass media, public forums, etc.;
• To communicate CRV concerns to Administration officials, Congressmen, economic leaders, and others who influence and determine U.S. policy.

The CRV is careful not to use the name of the Peace Corps in describing itself, and it does not limit its membership to former Peace Corps Volunteers. Anyone who has served in an overseas voluntary service program and who supports CRV's goals is eligible to join, but the overwhelming majority of members are former PCV's.

The CRV has undertaken a variety of projects. It sent a

Vietnam protest letter signed by 500 returnees to President
Johnson, agitated for sanctions against Rhodesia, organized
a speakers bureau, and stimulated discussions on a broad
range of issues dealing with the third world. The action
which attracted the most nationwide attention was the publication of a CRV position paper on Vietnam in the September,
1967 issue of *Ramparts* magazine. The document appeared
only three months after the Bruce Murray case had sensitized
most Peace Corps Volunteers to the implications of the Vietnam war. It appears to have had an important impact on
thinking about the Corps, for it raised some fundamental
questions. "We began to realize," said the position paper,
"that there are ambiguities inherent in United States-spon-
sored programs like the Peace Corps. Although its name
indicates a goal of serving the forces of peaceful change,
we wonder whether the Peace Corps' effect has not at times
been to impede rather than accelerate the movement into a
future of greater abundance and full political participation."

CRV has also entertained considerable discussion about
internationalizing the Peace Corps, although this is not part
of its stated program. In early 1968 a group of people in
and around CRV New York conceived of a plan to send a
mailing to all overseas Volunteers inviting them on July 4,
1968 to declare their individual severance from the Peace
Corps and affiliation with an international Peace Corps secretariat that was to be set up in Geneva. The decision of President Johnson not to seek re-election took the steam out of
this project, and the letters were never sent.

As of the summer of 1969 it appears that CRV is still
groping for an identity and a philosophy. Its most radicalized
leaders tend to dominate the internal dialogue, and this
discourages the more numerous moderates. Paradoxically,
Volunteers who spent two years trying to change attitudes in
the foreign cultures of Asia, Africa, and Latin America, now

find themselves at a loss as to how to go about changing attitudes in their own homeland. As a group, their most outstanding characteristic is their inability to agree on very much of anything. This quality was noted at the Washington returned Volunteers conference. A questionnaire that had been sent out to Volunteers revealed that the greatest agreement on any one question was less than 15 per cent. One of the questions asked how their resources could be harnessed, and "the most common reply was that harnessing was the last thing they wanted." [11] Apparently, "doing one's own thing" has reached the status of dogma among Volunteers to the point of excluding effective unity on political issues.

On several occasions Jack Vaughn was asked whether the war in Vietnam had hurt the Peace Corps and he invariably replied that it had had no effect. "The war in Vietnam has had no significant effect on our application input," he told the House Appropriations Committee in 1968. [12] Given the Murray case, the CRV position paper, and the criticism of the Peace Corps on college campuses, it is hard to believe that Vaughn does not know that this is nonsense. The statistics on Peace Corps applications are also revealing.

Program Year	Applications
1962	20,058
1963	33,762
1964	45,653
1965	39,957
1966	40,827
1967	34,046
1968	31,111

The high water mark was reached in 1964, just before the escalation of the war in Vietnam. Applications declined every year but one after that. Projections of future Volunteer strength have had to be scaled down regularly. In the spring of 1968 Vaughn told the House Appropriations committee that he expected a total for that year of 38,000 applications, of which an expected 26,190 would be invited to join, of which an expected 11,000 would actually accept and enter training. The figures turned out to be 31,111 applications, 16,301 invitations, and 7,278 acceptances.

It is, of course, impossible to prove that the Vietnam war is responsible for this decline, although I have yet to find a Volunteer or Peace Corps official who privately will not concede the relationship. However, in one way, the war aids recruitment, for the Corps can provide temporary shelter from the draft. Although they might not admit it publicly or on a questionnaire, many young men join up because many draft boards will grant a 2A occupational deferment for Peace Corps service. There have been cases of Volunteers being drafted, but these are rare. The consequence of this situation is that some men who have pretty radical and even anti-Peace Corps attitudes actually join the organization, and they have the effect of radicalizing others.

In any case, whether because of the relationship of the Peace Corps to the draft, or because of the educational effect of long term exposure to a foreign culture, many former Volunteers look upon their Corps experience as a "radicalizing" experience. They are not very clear about what they mean by this, although most often it relates to disillusionment about the role of the United States in world affairs in general and in developing areas in particular. On the other hand there is some evidence, particularly from completion of service evaluation conferences, that overseas service produces something akin to a colonial mentality. I have seen a report of one such conference in India which was primarily concerned with the negative feelings the Volunteers had about Indians, although it was very much to their credit that they were honest about these feelings, regretted them, and tried to figure out why they came to acquire them. Americans who believe in the achievement ethic, efficiency, frankness, informality, and other values of the American culture, may, during their Peace Corps experience, acquire contempt for foreigners who appear to them to be lazy, fatalistic, superstitious and devious. It happened to some of the British in India, and it may well happen to Americans there and elsewhere as well. If they allow this to show while they are overseas, they will certainly be unsuitable for the Peace Corps.

In the early days there was a magic about the Peace Corps that captured the imagination, not only of naive idealists, but of practical bureaucrats, and pragmatic politicians. It was due in part to the Kennedy mystique, to the extraordinary elan and administrative skill of Sargent Shriver, and to the outpouring of idealism among young people who sincerely wanted to make the world a better place. But the world cannot be made better by magic nor by naive idealism. Above all, it cannot be made better without a plan based upon valid theory. The Peace Corps was strong on magic, but weak on theory. Without the Vietnam war it might have developed, through trial and error, some theory and a workable program, but the Vietnam war amplified the contradiction between the interests of the United States and the interests of poor people. It made dedicated and idealistic young men like Bruce Murray unsuitable as representatives of the United States, and it is likely that such men will continue to be unsuitable for a considerable time to come.

IX: NIXON'S POLICIES

"In the long run the primary and preferred source
of capital for newly-developing countries must and should
be private investment rather than government loans and
grants. That is why our new developmental loan fund will
be channelled into private investment where possible. That
is why also government policies must be developed which
will encourage United States private investment in these
areas. And that is one of the reasons why our policies must
also encourage greatly expanded trade so that a pattern
of commerce with the free rather than the Communist
world will be established with these countries."

*Richard M. Nixon, then Vice President,
in a speech in the National Association
of Manufacturers on December 6, 1967.*

When Richard Nixon entered the White House he was
supposed to have had a plan for ending the war in Vietnam
and for attacking the problems of poverty and racial conflict
at home. But as his first year in office wore on, no plans
emerged very clearly and his policies on a broad range of
issues seemed ambiguous or confused.

While the Nixon foreign policy is virtually indistinguishable from that of his predecessor, there are some signs of
change in the Peace Corps. The changes are not fundamental
and do not alter the basic function of the organization as an
instrument of U.S. foreign policy. They are essentially
changes in style. Under Nixon the patina of romantic idealism
which the Peace Corps acquired from the Kennedy period
has been replaced with a businesslike shine. It is less appealing, but probably more honest.

The man President Nixon selected to head the Peace Corps
is 34 year-old Joseph H. Blatchford, an amiable and hand-
some man whose career suggests he possesses considerable
ability and a powerful ambition.

Born in Milwaukee in 1934, Blatchford attended high
school in Beverly Hills, California, and studied political

science at UCLA. He competed in championship tennis at Wimbledon in 1956 and served as a Second Lieutenant in the United States Army in Kentucky. In 1957 he enrolled in Boalt Law School at the University of California in Berkeley. The following year he was disturbed by the hostile reception that the then Vice-President Nixon received in Caracas, and decided to leave school and do something about it by organizing a student goodwill tour of Latin America. According to his Peace Corps biography, "the seven students in his touring troupe relied on tennis exhibitions and jazz as entrees to the Latin student community." Between March and June, 1959 they visited 30 cities. The following autumn he conceived the idea of a private peace corps which he called ACCION, the Spanish word for action. It began in 1967 with 40 American volunteers in Venezuela on a budget of $160,-000 donated by "24 corporations in the United States and Venezuela." According to Blatchford's biography: "ACCION had more than 1,000 field workers and staff members from nine countries in its first eight years. More than 3,000 companies contributed nearly $9,000,000 in cash and services during that time. There were more than 45,000 projects in four countries."

At first ACCION concentrated its efforts in rural areas, but gradually it moved into the cities. It had projects in Brazil, Peru, and Argentina as well as in Venezuela. ACCION claimed it was not a North American operation, but truly international. For example, it said that there was only one non-Venezuelan among the 70 field workers in Venezuela. Each country project was supposed to be autonomous and national in character.

In 1965 Blatchford set up ACCION International in New York City to support existing programs and develop new ones. It provided "seed money" for projects which were supposed to become self-supporting and self-directed. The head of the board of ACCION International was Donald M. Kendall, president of Pepsi Cola.

In 1968 Blatchford took a leave of absence as executive director of ACCION International in order to run for Congress in California's 17th Congressional District. He was narrowly defeated by the former Lieutenant Governor, Glenn Anderson, a Democrat. Blatchford keeps in touch with the district and local Democrats suspect he may run again.

It is obvious that whatever else it may be ACCION is the child of big business. It is clearly a public relations agency designed to promote a climate favorable for American interests in Latin America. That its founder and head should be appointed to take over the Peace Corps suggests that President Nixon sees little difference in the missions of the two organizations. The fact is that there is not much difference.

When Blatchford took over he inherited many problems and controversies. Not long after he assumed office the question of possible ties with the CIA was raised. In the spring of 1967, according to a *New York Post* article of March 29, 1969, Peace Corps Volunteers in Venezuela were instructed not to have any dealings with ACCION, apparently because of suspected CIA connections. And in May, 1969, Drew Pearson and Jack Anderson charged that ACCION had "accepted money from at least two CIA fronts." Blatchford immediately issued a detailed and persuasive denial, and subsequently Pearson and Anderson published a retraction stating "we are convinced that the Peace Corps has no connection, direct or indirect, with the CIA." They had erroneously charged that ACCION had received $50,000 from the Donner Foundation, a reported CIA conduit. "We now find," they said, "that there are two Donner Foundations and that the William H. Donner Foundation, which contributed to ACCION, has never been a CIA conduit."

The CIA issue came up again in August when a Communist

Deputy in Chile, Luis Figueroa, charged that Volunteers were engaged in espionage activities. On August 6, 1969, the Chilean Chamber of Deputies authorized its foreign relations committee to investigate. The charges were not proved, and Peace Corps effectiveness in Chile does not appear to have been seriously damaged. The event was apparently a rather clumsy effort to discredit the Corps without any sound basis in fact.

Another problem inherited by Blatchford had to do with Micronesia. On August 30, 1969 the *New Republic* carried an article by Paula Stern charging that the Peace Corps was phasing out twelve volunteer lawyers because of pressure from the Pentagon which wanted to establish new bases in the Islands. According to the article, Volunteer lawyers were helping the natives file legal complaints against the U. S. authorities, and Lieutenant General Lewis Walt of the Marine Corps blamed Fred Schulz, Peace Corps lawyer-adviser to the Palauian legislature, for a resolution passed by that body opposing an American base on Palau.

In a letter to the editor of the *New Republic*, Blatchford stated that the article was "based on totally false premises." "The fact is," he said, "that neither the Department of Defense nor any other agency has ever made such a demand on me, or implied such a demand, in any form. Eight lawyers are now serving in Micronesia and are due to stay until they complete their regular two-year tours of duty in June of 1970 . . . Had Miss Stern checked more closely she would have found that the lawyers' program has been under fire from the Peace Corps itself. Dissatisfaction with the entire Micronesia program has existed here since long before I arrived on the scene."

It is undeniable that political consciousness is rising in Micronesia at a time when the Pentagon, worried about being forced out of Okinawa, is thinking about making greater use

of the islands of the trust territory. The role that the Peace
Corps may have had in developing this consciousness is a
subject worth investigating. It would not be inconsistent with
its role as a sort of colonial civil service to oppose encroach-
ments by the military or educate the local inhabitants concerning their legal rights as subjects of the "mother country".

Perhaps the most important issue to confront Blatchford
when he assumed the directorship was the contention between
two basic schools of thought about what the Peace Corps
was and what it was supposed to be doing. One school conceived the agency as an idealistic group of young people
whose main task was to educate and organize poor people
for social change and economic improvement through self-
help. The emphasis was on teaching new attitudes, promoting
enthusiasm for innovation, dispelling lethargy and hopeless-
ness. The best Volunteers for such an approach were young
college graduates who would accept the hardship of living
and working with poor people, learn their language, and
identify with them.

The other school of thought saw the Peace Corps as an
agency for the dissemination of know-how necessary to development and modernization. Volunteers should be primarily experienced professionals who could teach indigenous
inhabitants the skills needed for economic progress. According to this school, host countries resented the well-meaning,
but incompetent amateurism of the A.B. generalists who did
not contribute much to the solution of economic problems.
Therefore, the Peace Corps should recruit older, more experienced professionals whose competence would command
respect and who could make a significant contribution to development.

These schools of thought coexisted within the agency from
the beginning, but the first was always dominant. For a
variety of reasons it was primarily A.B. generalists who were

recruited as volunteers. Thus the Peace Corps was essentially young, enthusiastic, idealistic, and frequently rambunctious.

From the moment he took over the directorship, there was little doubt that Blatchford belonged to the professionalist school, and he immediately set about remolding the agency to make it less amateurish. His first important action was to revamp the entire system of pay for Volunteers. He increased the basic allowances and gave the Volunteers more freedom on how they could spend their money. Such services as the handling of unaccompanied baggage were eliminated. Prohibitions against Volunteers spending their vacations in Western Europe or the United States were removed. The Volunteer was put more on his own. "Not only will large amounts of time be saved for Volunteers and staff by consolidation of these payments," said Blatchford in a memorandum to all country directors, "but more important, it will be made clear to the Volunteers that we regard them as serious, job-oriented workers, to be treated as responsible individuals."

Blatchford also added a new category to the regulation on early termination: "Termination for the convenience of the Peace Corps." "This category," he said, "will include Volunteers who do not or cannot perform well enough to justify their continued presence in the host country, and will also include those who are dismissed because their active misbehavior or violation of Peace Corps policies and regulations make their continued presence undesirable." Volunteers terminated for these reasons would receive free transportation home and would have the right to appeal the decision to the director. All of these measures seemed designed to make it easier to recruit older people with professional experience and to dismiss Volunteers who turned out to be incompetent.

Blatchford certainly did not intend to eliminate the A.B. generalists. He merely wanted to increase the proportion of more mature, experienced professionals. Whether his recruitment efforts would be successful could not be determined during his first year, and as of September, 1969, his office could offer no evidence one way or another. Blatchford had high hopes of cooperation from business and trade unions in offering incentives and job security to potential Volunteers.

The new director took office at a difficult time in American politics. He showed that he was aware of this in his statement to the Senate Foreign Relations Committee when he enumerated the country's difficulties: "turmoil on the campuses with no end in sight; a polarization of our society; America's disillusionment with America's role in the world, symbolized by the reduction of foreign assistance; increasing distrust with the motives of our Government; and frustration at the apparent inability of any government to solve basic problems."[1] But he still described the Peace Corps as nonpolitical, "an altruistic expression of America's good intentions toward the world — our desire to help, our will to serve mankind." "Morever," he told his country directors, "the Peace Corps comes without strings or ulterior motive, separate from American foreign policy, with no other purpose than to help where neded."[2]

There were signs that this characterization was no longer credible. One was the growth and increasing radicalization of the Committee of Returned Volunteers (CRV). In June, 1969, a representative of the New York chapter, Marcella Kerr, appeared before the Senate Foreign Relations Committee to complain about the Peace Corps handling of the Bruce Murray case. She asked that the committee "carefully investigate this case because its implications are both numerous and far reaching." "The Peace Corps," she added, "is political not only in its origin and structure but also in its functions." She suggested that its original ideals might best be served by transforming it into an organ of an international body such as the United Nations. Her testimony put

the agency somewhat on the defensive, and for the first time
it produced a detailed statement on the Murray case.

Meanwhile, the CRV itself became more and more radical
and hostile to the government. It increasingly saw itself as a
component of "the movement", that loose amalgam of new
left forces ranging from SDS to the Black Panthers. In the
summer of 1969 it sent two delegations to Cuba. Among them
were former Volunteers who had served in Latin America
and who had the language skills and the experience with
which to evaluate the modernization process in Cuba. The
September, 1969 CRV Newsletter contained a brief set of
impressions by one of the members of the group, Bonnie
Packer, formerly with the Peace Corps in Turkey. It was a
laudatory report but it was clear that the delegation had not
abandoned its critical faculties:

"We had many opportunities to gather information and
impressions about the educational system, about land usage
and agricultural production and about the spirit of the youth
—how this spirit is developed and maintained. We gathered
more sketchy information about the distribution of power,
about economic distribution, about the allocation of justice,
principally because these are areas which are still developing and which still have many problems. We raised many
questions about the long lines and the empty stores, the nature
of social equality, the position of blacks and of women, the
meaning of materialism, traditional education, civil liberties,
etc."

Finally Miss Packer concluded: "We learned to appreciate
that radicals have a role in the U. S. to undermine the
capitalist structure so that not only would imperialism be
destroyed at home, but would also be destroyed in the third
world. In a certain sense, the peoples of the third world
look to the radicals in the U.S. to help them, not by coming
to fight in the mountains but to do our revolutionary thing

here. We had a vision of imperialism being attacked from all sides."

This radical mood dominated the CRV General Assembly held near Minneapolis in September, 1969. In a position paper on the Peace Corps CRV attacked the agency for supporting the status quo in countries to which it sends volunteers. It detailed the ways in which this was done and said: "We have come to the unavoidable conclusion that the Peace Corps should be abolished. . ."

There are reasons to question whether the leftward movement of the CRV is representative of the over 30,000 Volunteers who have returned from Peace Corps service. Most of them have not joined CRV. Many who have, do not play an active role, and local chapters report a big turnover in attendance at meetings. Moreover, numerous returned Volunteers have not only gone to work for government agencies, but several hundred of them, according to Deputy Director Brent K. Ashabranner, "have chosen quite of their own volition to work in the AID program in Vietnam. They do, in many cases, the same kinds of grassroots level work with the people that they were able to do in their Peace Corps service. In other words, they are utilizing in Vietnam the kind of skills, development skills, that they acquired in their Peace Corps service, and they have undertaken this work purely because they wanted to."[3] While some returned Volunteers try to "undermine the the capitalist structure" at home, others are willing to help reinforce it abroad, even in Vietnam. It is still too early to determine on which side of the contest the main weight of the returned Volunteers will be felt.

The direction being taken by the Peace Corps under Nixon and Blatchford is not entirely new. It was set under Johnson and Vaughn. Blatchford may produce a Peace Corps that is more "professional" and less troublesome. It will gear in more smoothly with other instruments of U.S. foreign policy, particularly AID and USIA. But it is unlikely that it will be a magnet for idealists. Thus, under Nixon, we may witness the decline of Macaulayism.

This, in my opinion, would be a good thing, for it is Macaulayism that casts an aura of legitimacy over U.S. expansionism and makes this dangerous phenomenon more effective. For a Republican administration, openly committed to the expansion of American business interests abroad, to preside over the liquidation of one of expansionism's major assets in the developing world, would constitute a poetic irony that would certainly make Che Guevara smile.

X: FUTURE OF THE PEACE CORPS

"The human and material resources that make a great society are produced at home, not abroad. An ambitious foreign policy built on a deteriorating domestic base is possible only for a limited time; like the light cast by an extinct star, it is predestined to come to an end. Such, approximately, was the experience of France before the war of 1870 and of Austria before the war of 1914. America is nowhere near that extremity but she will come to it eventually if we do not stop to put our own house in order, or, more exactly, if we do not resume the work of educating our children, combating poverty, renewing our cities, and purifying our physical environment begun so hopefully by Presidents Kennedy and Johnson."

Senator J. William Fulbright,
The Arrogance of Power, p. 217.

It should be clear from the foregoing chapters that the Peace Corps is an instrument of United States foreign policy. Confusion on this point derives primarily from the fact that the Corps' effectiveness in serving American interests abroad depends in large measure on creating the illusion that it has some other purpose. "The Peace Corps," said Secretary of State Dean Rusk in a peculiar mixture of deception and frankness, "is not an instrument of foreign policy, because to make it so would rob it of its contribution to foreign policy." It is the contribution to foreign policy that counts with the White House, the State Department, and the Congress, and this is the basis on which volunteers, potential volunteers, and the general public should evaluate the Peace Corps, and decide whether or not to support it.

As I have shown in Chapter II, the foreign policy of the United States is to expand economically, culturally, and where necessarily, militarily. Such expansionism is not new in history or unique to the United States. All great powers tend to be expansionist. Russia, both before and since the Revolution, has been expansionist. Depending upon one's view of the history of sovereignty in Tibet, Mongolia, and Sinkiang, China is also expansionist. Even small states like Israel are expansionist when they can get away with it. Powerful nations tend to use their power to dominate those areas of the world that can be useful to them. They try to establish spheres of influence, and such areas frequently become spheres of exploitation. Eastern Europe and the Caribbean are good examples.

It has been customary among academic political scientists in the United States to avoid passing moral judgments on this phenomenon. Great powers expand, the political scientists have said. It is a fact of life. We might wish they did not, but they do, and that is that.

I cannot agree with this so-called "objective" and "ethically neutral" point of view. That the strong tend to dominate the weak does not mean that we should concede that might is right. If it is wrong for the strong to dominate the weak, I believe we should say so, and turn our attention to devising techniques to prevent it. This indeed is what Western man did when he established the institution of law and the concept of equity. That law has been perverted in some countries to serve only the rich does not, in my opinion, invalidate law as a device for protecting the weak against unfair treatment by the strong. Without law we have a jungle in which the weak perish. With law there is some hope of security for those who may not be strong, but who may be the carriers of values that civilized men want to preserve—gentleness, kindness, artistry, and good manners.

The arena of international relations has always been a jungle despite brave efforts, beginning perhaps in the 16th century with Hugo Grotius, to rise above it. The United States, notably under Woodrow Wilson, has tried to contribute to the building of an international legal system that would provide for the pacific settlement of disputes. Most

American presidents have given at least lip service to the idea. It was on these grounds that President Dwight Eisenhower opposed the Anglo-French-Israeli invasion of Egypt in 1956. "There can be no peace without law," he said. "And there can be no law if we work to invoke one code of international conduct for those who oppose, and another for our friends. . . . The peace we seek and need means much more than mere absence of war. It means the acceptance of law and the fostering of justice in all the world."

President Johnson, when he asked Arthur Goldberg to leave the Supreme Court and become Ambassador to the United Nations, renewed the commitment to a rule of law. "We strive," he said, "for a world where all men may live in peace with the hope of justice under the rule of law over the conduct of nations. Committed as we are to this principle and this purpose, it is fitting that we should ask a member of our highest court to relinquish that office to speak for America before the nations of the world."

In my opinion this is good doctrine, but it was never really U.S. policy. Eisenhower, in violation of international law, sent Francis Gary Powers to fly his U-2 over the Soviet Union. Kennedy, in violation of international law, invaded Cuba with a proxy army, and later when Cuba permitted the installation of ballistic missiles on her soil (which she had every legal right to do, just as Turkey had done with American missiles), Kennedy threatened the Soviet Union with nuclear war unless the missiles were withdrawn. Johnson, in violation of international law, bombed North Vietnam, invaded the Dominican Republic, and authorized the use of gas warfare in Vietnam, among other illegalities. The record in recent years has been one of contempt for international law and shameful hypocrisy.

In condemning the illegal behavior of the United States, one should not turn a blind eye toward that of other nations.

The illegal Soviet interventions in Hungary and Czechoslo-
vakia, and the Chinese invasion of India are just as repre-
hensible. One suspects that the record of these two giants
would be even worse were they not restrained by their limited
economic resources and by the threat of war with the United
States.

However, the United States gives particular cause for concern simply because it is by far the most powerful. The
capacity of the United States to expand, coupled with its
willingness to violate international law, produces a threat to
world stability of extraordinary proportions. The American
people are energetic, talented, persistent, aggressive, and
messianic. They are also capable of a frightening barbarism,
as the Vietnam war has made clear to all who are willing
to look at the evidence. By what right can they claim to
police the world? On what basis should anyone think they
would do it more humanely than any other major power?

Yet it is clear that the idea that the United States should
police the world is not simply the fantasy of right wing
fanatics, but the responsible opinion of respected American
statesmen. Charles W. Yost, U.S. Ambassador to the United
Nations, is a good example. Yost was the Deputy U.S. Representative to the United Nations from 1961 to 1966. He
has also served as U.S. Ambassador to Laos, Syria, and Morocco. *Foreign Affairs,* the most prestigious of "establishment" journals in the field of international relations, gave
feature billing to an article by Yost in its October, 1968,
issue. It was entitled "World Order and American Responsibility," and it argued that the United States and the Soviet
Union should get together to police the world, but if that
were not possible, then the United States should go it alone.
"One's reluctant conclusion," said Yost, "is that over the
next decade the effective responsibility for international security may rest very largely with the United States and the

U.S.S.R. either in competition or cooperation, or more likely in some untidy combination of the two. What does this actually mean in practice? It probably means, first, that in case serious international disorder is provoked by communist states, parties, or movements, the United States, if it considers that this disorder threatens its own 'vital' interests or those of an ally, will have either to work out with the Soviet Union an agreed means of checking or limiting it, or act against it more or less unilaterally with only such help as the state or states directly concerned can supply."

Another world policeman of this general type is Samuel P. Huntington, Chairman of the Department of Government at Harvard University and a consultant to the Department of State and AID. Huntington has called for a new government agency charged with intervening politically in the developing nations to construct governments and political parties that would indirectly serve the American interest. "What we could use, perhaps," he wrote, "is a new-style CIA, more skilled in building governments than in subverting them." Huntington said that political intervention might promote stable governments and then military intervention would not be necessary. "Such a program of preventive political involvement," he said, "would be less visible to both the American public and foreign publics."[1] Presumably the advantage in this low visibility is that people would be less likely to complain if they did not know what was going on. Perhaps some former Peace Corps Volunteers would be ideal recruits for the new-style CIA.

It is not surprising that Yost and Huntington, and other American expansionists see U.S. military and political interventionism as a form of disinterested public service which the rich perform because only they can afford it. This is self-delusion. The United States exercises police power to protect the interests of those who control the American gov-

ernment. There is no altruism. Neither is there any legitimacy, for the policing role is grounded neither in law nor
on the consent of those policed.

Even in this day of rapid communication and world-wide
news reporting, most Americans know very little about international affairs. They are interested only in the big stories,
and they learn about them only superficially. Domestic
affairs, as they do in every nation, claim most of their attention. The consequence of this situation is that foreign policy
does not receive the critical scrutiny that domestic policies
do. Foreign affairs become the domain of elites that function
behind a curtain of public ignorance.

The elites which determine America's role in world affairs
are based in American business, in the gigantic corporations
that dominate the United States political economy. A new
generation of academic scholars, inspired by the pioneering
of the late C. Wright Mills, is documenting this phenomenon
in impressive detail.[2] But it is not necessary to turn to their
work to see what is happening. The journals of the business
community provide plenty of evidence. They show the
emergence of new classes of rich people in America who
grow richer and more powerful as the lower classes struggle
to retain what little they have. In the May, 1968, *Fortune*
magazine, Jeremy Main, in a well researched article, spoke
of the people who earn $25,000 a year or more as "the spear-
head of a mass movement." "In 1950," he wrote, "only
303,000 individual couples had a taxable income of more
than $25,000. By 1960, the number had risen to 567,000.
This spring an estimated 1,373,000 tax returns were filed
reporting incomes of $25,000 or more. By the end of the
century one out of four Americans probably will be earning
$25,000 or more a year."

The same issue of *Fortune* carried another article entitled
"America's Centimillionaires," by Arthur M. Louis. "The

U. S. has become so affluent," said Louis, "that there no longer is any great prestige in being a mere millionaire. The very word 'millionaire' is seldom used nowadays; indeed, it has an almost quaint sound. . . . To have a net worth of [only] $1 million today is to be, much of the time, indistinguishable from members of the omnipresent middle class." The article said there were 153 individuals in the U.S. today whose net worth amounted to $100 million or more.

While millionaires are becoming commonplace and those who earn $25,000 a year are becoming a "mass movement," other Americans go hungry. In December, 1968, anthropologist Margaret Mead told a Senate Committee that almost ten million Americans get inadequate nourishment and "many of these are on the verge of starvation." "Today," she said, "we seem unable to deal with poverty, in spite of our greatly increased productivity and far greater technical resources."

The issue of course is not capability but intent; not what American decision-makers can do, but what they prefer to do. According to the originally secret Wood-McClintock report prepared at the direction of the Johnson administration and made available to Congress by President Nixon, the United States spends between $4 and $5-billion annually to maintain 429 major and 2,972 minor military bases scattered throughout the world. This is what the decision makers prefer to do. Why do they spend this staggering sum on military bases overseas and not on food for hungry people at home? They do it in the name of defense, but one must ask defense of whom from what? With thousands of nuclear tipped missiles in submarines and secure silos capable of utterly destroying any nation that attacks our homeland, why do we need more than 3,000 bases overseas? They cannot be explained as necessary to defense of our homeland; they can only be explained as a world-wide police force. The United States would rather police the whole world than feed its own people.

What is the reason for such a grotesque ordering of priorities?

The rich and the super rich control the giant corporations which, through lobbies, through campaign contributions, through appointments, and thousands of other devices, control the American government and its foreign policy. The wealth and power of these corporations is staggering. General Motors, for example, handles more money annually than the gross national product of all but seventeen nations of the world.[3] As these gigantic corporations spread out over the globe they become, in many ways, more powerful and influential than the nation-states in which they operate. Indeed, so much power is shifting away from the state to the corporation, that some men are thinking of redesigning the international system to make it the primary actor in world affairs.

Like most high officials of the present administration, former U.S. Ambassador to the United Nations, George Ball, is a frank advocate of "more power to the corporations." Prior to accepting the U.N. post, Ball was a senior partner in Lehman Brothers, an investment firm, and in that capacity made an important speech to the British National Committee of the International Chamber of Commerce in London. An abridged version of the speech was printed in the magazine *War/Peace Report* for October, 1968. Ball argued that the political boundaries of nation-states have become too narrow and constrictive for modern business, and that ways must be found to free the corporations from national laws that impede their growth. This is desirable because the world corporation, after all, is "the best means yet devised for using world resources according to the criterion of profit, which is an objective standard of efficiency." Ball says that corporations should become "quite literally citizens of the world." This could be accomplished by a treaty called an "International Companies Law" which "could well place limitations, for example, on the restrictions that a nation-state might be permitted to impose on companies established under its sanction." Ball insists he is not proposing a world government, but that "freeing commerce from national inter- ference through the creation of new world instrumentalities would inevitably, over time, help to stimulate mankind to close the gap between the archaic political structure of the world and the visions of commerce which vault beyond con- fining national boundaries to exploit the full promise of the world economy."

The political thought of George Ball and men like him appears to be aimed toward a world in which national sov- ereignties wither away and political and economic power is monopolized by international corporations. This may not be utterly fantastic. Arthur Barber, former deputy assistant sec- retary of defense, estimates that within a generation about 400 to 500 international corporations will own about two-thirds of the fixed assets of the world.[4] If they own so much, it is reasonable to expect that they will want to run things, even more than they already do.

According to Ball, the international corporation of the future may have a home base in a particular country, but gradually "share ownership in the parent [company] must be widely dispersed so that the company cannot be regarded as the exclusive instrument of a particular nation." He also says that there should be a "gradual internationalizing of boards of directors and parent company managements."[5]

One of the remarkable things about this analysis is that it conforms so closely to the Marxist model. As early as 1848 in the *Communist Manifesto*, Marx and Engels described the emergence of an international class of the rich who would restructure economic and political power on a global scale, breaking down national boundaries in the process. Three paragraphs of this hoary document read almost as if they had been written about men like George Ball.

"The need of a constantly expanding market for its products chases the bourgeoisie [read: the modern corporation]
over the whole surface of the globe. It must nestle everywhere, settle everywhere, establish connections everywhere.

"The bourgeoisie has through its exploitation of the world
market given a cosmopolitan character to production and
consumption in every country. To the great chagrin of re-
actionaries, it has drawn from under the feet of industry
the national ground on which it stood. All old-established
national industries have been destroyed or are daily being
destroyed. They are dislodged by new industries, whose introduction becomes a life and death question for all civilized
nations, by industries that no longer work up indigenous
raw material, but raw material drawn from the remotest
zones; industries whose products are consumed, not only at
home, but in every quarter of the globe. In place of the old
wants, satisfied by the production of the country, we find new
wants, requiring for their satisfaction the products of distant
lands and climes. In place of the old local and national se-
clusion and self-sufficiency, we have intercourse in every
direction, universal interdependence of nations. . . .

"The bourgeosie, by the rapid improvement of all instruments of production, by the immensely facilitated means of
communication, draws all nations, even the most barbarian,
into civilization. The cheap prices of its commodities are the
heavy artillery with which it batters down all Chinese walls,
with which it forces the barbarians' intensely obstinate hatred
of foreigners to capitulate. It compels all nations, on pain
of extinction, to adopt the bourgeois mode of production;
it compels them to introduce what it calls civilization into
their midst, i.e., to become bourgeois themselves. In a word,
it creates a world after its own image."

According to Karl Marx, Friedrich Engels, and spokesmen
of recent American administrations, the internationalization

and global expansion of business is the central feature of world affairs. For all three it is a progressive step which breaks down archaic political and economic structures and moves human organization to a higher stage. Marx and Engels, of course, were not willing to stop there, for they believed that while this new arrangement was better than the old, it worked primarily to the advantage of the rich and increased the exploitation of the poor. The doctrine of Communism was invented, therefore, to change this. It provided for a strategy wherein the poor were to unite on a world-wide basis, as the rich had done. The watchwords were: international proletarian solidarity. Unfortunately, from the Communists' point of view, it has been much more difficult for the poor to organize across national boundaries than it has been for the rich, and nationalism has been a better weapon with which to oppose the expanding corporation than internationalism. The conflict between the government of Peru and the International Petroleum Corporation is a good example.

It is an article of faith among Black Power militants and student radicals that the relationship of Black communities to the White power structure is essentially colonial.[*] In this classic Marxist-Leninist interpretation the struggle for Black liberation is seen as a part of the world-wide revolution against the power structure that is responsible for American expansionism. The Viet Cong, the Black Panthers, and the Students for a Democratic Society become natural allies, and the romantic figure of Che Guevara emerges as a universal symbol of the courage of the oppressed in the struggle against the rich. Unfortunately for the poor, their capacity to organize and make alliances is still inferior to that of the rich. While Marxist theory has some utility for description, it has proved less useful as a guide to strategy.

There are no theories of international politics that explain

all observable behavior of nations and statesmen, or that
enable one to predict the actions of all of the actors in the
world arena. Similarly, any view of politics that sees the
world as inhabited only by "the good guys and the bad guys"
is naive and dangerous. But a desire not to oversimplify or
distort should not be allowed to prevent the identification of
salient features that make world affairs easier to understand.

In my opinion, the most important element of world affairs
today is the growing economic gap between the rich and the
poor and the consequent development of world wide political
conflict between them. The internationalization of that conflict occasioned by the growing solidarity among the rich on
the one hand and to a lesser degree, among the poor on the
other, has by no means obliterated national boundaries,
national interests, or nationalism. The main reason for this
is that the proportion of wealth to poverty is not the same
in all nations. To some extent the distribution of wealth corre-
sponds to national boundaries, and therefore there are such
things as rich nations that join together to perpetuate their
wealth.

It is this phenomenon which, more than anything else,
explains the detente between the U.S. and the U.S.S.R. The
Soviet Union is now relatively rich. The old doctrines of
Communism are no longer necessary, and indeed are being
cited primarily by the Chinese to show how far the Russians
have deviated from Marxism-Leninism. Increasing Soviet
wealth and the conservatism that goes with it are what makes
it reasonable for a Charles Yost to hope for Russo-American
cooperation as the world's policemen.

As the world is becoming polarized between the rich and
the poor, the Peace Corps is found on the side of the rich.
It serves the interests of the richest nation under the guise
of helping the poor. But the help it gives to the poor is truly
minimal. This judgment is strengthened by the findings of

a recent book on the Peace Corps, *Agents of Change,* by David Hapgood and Meridan Bennett (Boston: Little Brown, 1968). Hapgood and Bennett have served in the Peace Corps as program evaluators, between the two of them evaluating seventeen programs and visiting many more. In researching the book they received considerable help from the Peace Corps and access to documents not available to outside scholars. They insist, however, that their book is "anything but official."

While *Agents of Change* does contain a considerable amount of critical comment, it is certainly a pro-Peace Corps book. Indeed, it is probably the most sophisticated defense of the Peace Corps available. Its effectiveness lies in the fact that it concedes the major point that is made most often by critics, namely that the Corps does not really make much of a dent in poverty. "As a contributor to development in the third world," say Hapgood and Bennett, "the Peace Corps can make no great claims to accomplishment. . . . Volunteers have filled a lot of jobs, but their utility in those jobs, and often the utility of the jobs themselves, is questionable." (p. 219). But while the Peace Corps is ineffective in development, it does not do much harm, they say, and it does benefit the United States:

". . . though they have not yet contributed much to development and their making of friends is beside any real point, the volunteers have justified John F. Kennedy's idea many times over by what they have learned. What they do with that learning in later years will be the measure of what the American people are getting for their money. In our opinion, we Americans are likely to draw high dividends from our investment in the Peace Corps. Americans are getting a very special kind of education at a bargain price; this is the clearest result of the Peace Corps experiment." (p. 220).

I have heard this same argument from many former Volunteers. They concede that the Peace Corps does little good for the host country and may do harm, but they say that the educational advantage to Americans, the new attitudes and perspectives they acquire, are justification for its continuance. I think a closer look must be taken at the educational result as well as at the cost, not simply in money, but in long term political consequences.

There is hardly any systematically gathered data on changes in political attitudes and in world views experienced by Volunteers as a result of their service. We simply do not know whether they become better, more enlightened, socially conscious citizens, or not. There is some data furnished by the Peace Corps on what they do when they return to the United States. As of June 30, 1968, the Peace Corps had data on 10,281 former Volunteers. Of the total, 3844 or 37.4% were back in school continuing their education. Another 2035 were teaching. A total of 1154 were or had been working for the federal government as follows:[7]

Peace Corps	401
State Department	62
A.I.D.	219
U.S.I.A.	26
Other	446

It is significant, I think, that so many former Volunteers wished to make a career of serving U.S. foreign policy. It may very well be, as many in the Peace Corps assert, that Volunteers enter agencies like the State Department and AID in order to change conduct of American policy. But it is important to ask whether they serve to limit American expansionism or whether, like Macaulay in India, they simply humanize it a bit, and make it more palatable.

The same question can be asked about the Volunteers who return from overseas and go into the business world. As of

June 1968, the Peace Corps had information on 1260 who had done so. "The financial world," says a Peace Corps pamphlet on returned Volunteers, "also has attracted a substantial number of former Volunteers, particularly those firms with international ties. About 15 former Volunteers are employed by the First National City Bank of New York and 10 work for Bankers Trust Company."

Are these Volunteers inhibiting or aiding American expansionism? Numerically, they are not a large percentage of returned Volunteers, but their long range impact on American expansionism may nevertheless be significant. As Anthony M. Solomon, Assistant Secretary of State for Economic Affairs, told the House Foreign Affairs Committee in 1967, U.S. business thinks in long range terms. He said:

". . . in practice for many of the firms that make investments in developing countries—in my view, based on conversations with many of the men who run those firms—their motivation is frequently one of getting into what they believe and hope will eventually be a large market, looked at from a long-term point of view. That is, it is not the immediate profit considerations which are so attractive. Large firms have large volumes of earnings, which they don't know what to do with frequently, and there are times when they feel the domestic situation does not permit reinvestment of the mass of earnings they would like to see devoted to the company's expansion. Therefore, there will be a tendency to look abroad and frequently to make investments which would be justified from their point of view only on a long term basis."[8]

Obviously, former Peace Corps Volunteers, who know the cultures of these developing areas at the grass roots level, could be very useful to expansionist companies in developing and marketing products that indigenous populations would buy.

I believe that it is true, as Solomon said, that the larger

firms have large volumes of earnings that they do not know
what to do with. Why, it may be asked, do they not invest
these earnings in new enterprises in the Black communities
of the United States where the demand for capital is so great
and the supply so limited? The answer has to do with profit
and regulation; there is more of the former and less of the
latter abroad. The business of business, after all, is to make
money, not solve social problems. But this should not be the
business of the U.S. government, and certainly not the Peace
Corps.

It is argued, especially by some of the more sophisticated
members of the international business community, that there
is no fundamental conflict of interest between the expanding
international corporation and the poor people of developing
countries. On the contrary, they say, they have a common
interest in development. Modernization benefits both.

In principle, this is probably correct, but in practice the
issue is more complicated. One can find an analagous situation within the United States in the relationship between the
medical profession and the poor people who need, but cannot afford, medical care. It can truly be said that there is
no fundamental conflict of interest between the doctors who
dispense medical treatment and the poor people who need it.
Doctors need patients and the sick need doctors. Nevertheless, in the United States where we have some of the finest
doctors and the most advanced medical techniques in the
world, we also have millions of people who cannot afford
adequate medical care. One of the major reasons for this is
that the organized medical profession exerts tremendous
political pressure to prevent the passage of legislation that
would make inexpensive medical care available to everyone.
What happens is that the doctors create a conflict of interest
between themselves and their potential patients where there
need not be one. The result is that the doctors maintain a

special privileged position in the society, and the poor go without medical care.

Making medical care available to the poor in America is not simply a question of training more doctors or advancing science, although both are important and desirable. But more important is the development of a system of distribution of medical services based on need rather than the ability to pay. Similarly, the conquest of poverty in the developing areas is not simply a function of industrialization and modernization, although both are important. It requires the development of systems of distribution based on need, and just as the doctors constitute an obstacle to such developments in American medical care, so do American businesses constitute an obstacle to such developments in the poorer countries. The reason for this is that they inevitably become allied to indigenous privileged classes that refuse, for a variety of reasons, to allow the poor to share equitably in the benefits of modernization. This relationship is further reinforced by the ideology of anti-Communism and anti-Socialism that pervades American business and influences almost everything it does. Until this changes, it would be wise for the governments of developing areas to be cautious about allowing American business to take up positions in their economies, for once established it might be difficult to get them out without confronting the U.S. Marines.

While the Peace Corps does some good work abroad, while it does educate some Americans in ways that are socially valuable, it nevertheless seems to me, on balance, to be an instrument of American expansionism, and therefore a contributor to a phenomenon that endangers the peace and welfare of most of mankind. I believe that the Peace Corps strengthens the domination of the rich over the poor, perpetuates illusions about the true character of the United States' role in world affairs, and diverts youthful talents away from the tasks of domestic reconstruction and reform. What then should be done with it, and what tasks should be undertaken by groups like the CRV that genuinely want to help the poor and the oppressed?

There are many causes of poverty in the world—low agricultural production, technological backwardness, geography and the weather, among other things. But perhaps the most important and the most neglected causes of poverty are political. If the political system fails to direct governmental resources into the areas of greatest need, then there can be no effective attack on poverty until there is basic political change. The poverty we have in America, the wealthiest country in the world, is clearly political poverty. We have the technology, we have the capital. We could eliminate poverty almost instantly if we decided to do it. The reasons we do not do it are political. Our political and economic decision making process is controlled by the rich and is used to increase the wealth of the rich. Until this is changed, poverty will not disappear.

Does this mean there must be a revolution? If by revolution one means some simple notion of the workers banding together, overthrowing the government, liquidating the rich, and ushering in the dictatorship of the proletariat who will then create socialism, then I would not favor revolution and think it is romantic nonsense to advocate it. If by revolution one means breaking the stranglehold of the Southern Democrats on the Congress, abolishing lobbies, eliminating private financing of election campaigns, extending the franchise to eighteen-year olds, establishing a ceiling on incomes, guaranteeing free medical care and a minimum annual income for all citizens, then I am for a revolution. Most contemporary American "revolutionaries" would dismiss such changes as mere reformism, but I think they go beyond that, for if achieved they would profoundly alter the distribution of

political and economic power in the United States. They
would not reinforce an antiquated system, but in effect,
replace it with a new one. All of these are political goals
and can be achieved only by political means. In any case,
unless we achieve some of them, we are not likely to wrest
the government from the rich and give it over to the control
of the majority of the people.

Such a transfer of control of the apparatus of the state
from one group or class to a broader, more representative
segment of the population would certainly be resisted by the
rich and the privileged. In many countries, including the
United States, it need not be done, and probably cannot be
done, with violence and internal war. Still, in some of the
countries of the developing world, it probably cannot be
accomplished peacefully. Nevertheless, without such fundamental changes in the structure of power, poverty is very unlikely to be eliminated, simply because the rich do not care
to eliminate it.

If it is true, then, that the elimination of poverty depends
upon fundamental and revolutionary political change, one
cannot be a true "agent of change" without being involved
in politics. It is clear that Jack Vaughn understood this, and
had no intention of allowing Peace Corps Volunteers to be
involved in this way. In 1966 he told the Senate Foreign
Relations Committee:

"I have never suggested that the Peace Corps was going
to set revolutionary forces in motion. What we are talking
about, Senator, is getting people involved in local government, getting people involved and trained to participate effectively in local institutions, getting people to the point of
being effective citizens. Really, this in most underdeveloped
countries of the world is revolutionary because the people
have never participated before. They never had the institutions to participate in. So I don't think we are really talking

about unleashing revolutionary movements. We are talking
about building across the board in the villages, in the slums,
and in the towns democratic action, so that the people can
participate in their society and in their government." [9]

The emphasis here is on good citizenship by working within
the system, not trying to change it. It is political integration,
not change. Vaughn wanted to tie the poor more closely
to the system, not replace the system with one that was more
just. Put another way, the Peace Corps without really making
an impact on poverty encourages people to adjust to the
present configurations of political power. In political terms,
and therefore economically as well, the Peace Corps Volunteers are not agents of change, but agents of the status quo.

I think this is also true of what is called the domestic
Peace Corps; VISTA, Volunteers in Service to America. VISTA
takes great pains to be sure that its Volunteers are not agents
of political change. Even though, like the Peace Corps, VISTA
says it does not pay its Volunteers salaries, but rather "allowances," these pittances are enough to bring the Volunteers
under the Hatch Act which forbids political activity by government employees. Thus their work, like that of the Peace
Corps, is essentially ameliorative, not remedial.

A good example is the VISTA bail project in San Francisco
where Volunteers work with people who have been arrested
to arrange for them to be released on their own recognizance
without bail. This is of great help to the poor who cannot
afford bail, and saves the city thousands of dollars in food
and lodging costs of prisoners. But it does nothing to attack
the poverty in which the criminality is bred; it merely
strengthens the legal system that keeps the poor from explod-
ing into violence. To attack the poverty the rich would have
to be taxed and public spending priorities would have to be
changed. That would require the kind of political action
which is forbidden to VISTA Volunteers.

Just as political awareness is developing among Peace Corps Volunteers and returnees, there are also signs that it is appearing in VISTA. The September, 1968, issue of the *Vista Volunteers* carried an article by Steve Skinner which dealt with some of these issues. Skinner asked why there had been so little progress in fighting poverty in the United States. "It is because," he said, "we have been dealing with effects and not with causes. And the primary causes of poverty in affluent twentieth century America are simply these: racism and classism that inherently pervade almost every level and facet of white American society today. . . ." Skinner called for parallel movements—Blacks working with Blacks, Whites working with Whites. The middle and upper income Whites, he said, should no longer go into the ghettoes. Instead they should work on the causes of poverty. "They must deal with their own racism and classism, whether individual or institutional."

Skinner has singled out the two great evils of the United States, racism and classism. The existence of both are established beyond doubt by presidential commissions, scholarly studies, and the publications of the business elite such as *Fortune* and *Nation's Business*. They are found primarily in the middle and upper classes, and that is where they must be combatted. Therefore, to take idealistic change-oriented, middle class, young, people away from their own environments, and to send them overseas or into ghettoes and Indian reservations is to take them away from the people who most need to change.

The charter of the United Nations Educational, Scientific, and Cultural Organization states that since wars begin in the minds of men, it is in the minds of men that the defenses of peace must be constructed. If this is true, these questions follow: What is a war-like idea, and in the minds of which men is it most likely to arise? In my opinion, the idea that one nation-state has the right to intervene politically and militarily whenever and wherever it wants in the world is a war-like idea. There is probably no country where this idea is held by more people than in the United States, and therefore if one wishes to construct the defenses of peace, there is no better place to start than in the minds of the American people.

In the American middle class we have a dangerous mixture of racism, classism, and interventionism which helps to perpetuate world wide economic injustice and the constant threat of World War III. Here is where the agents of change are needed more than anywhere else. Here is where the skills of community development need to be exercised. Here is where Volunteers ought to be working. If it makes sense to put them in remote villages in foreign countries and expect them to teach school and organize a community in their spare time, then it does not seem unreasonable to put them in the cities and suburbs of America to teach school and organize the communities there.

In an important sense the United States is underdeveloped and backward. Its political institutions are no longer adequate to the demands being made on them, and its moral sensibilities seem atrophied around the concepts of self-interest and pragmatism. The country needs new leadership. It needs young people who will run for political office, it needs community developers who will get elected to school boards, it needs humanitarians who will enter the police forces, and imaginative teachers who will take over the schools. It needs bright young scholars who will expose and discredit the Huntingtons, the Yosts, the Balls, the Kristols and the other apologists for expansionism. It needs journalists who will defend the cause of truth against the pressures of advertisers, and film makers who will educate and inspire.

For the American people to turn their energies toward

domestic reform it is not necessary for them to become isolationists. Obviously, the United States cannot withdraw from world affairs; no great power can. But the curtailment of expansionism is not withdrawal, and opposition to the unhealthy domination of domestic and foreign policy by the rich and super rich is not neo-isolationism. In his famous Mr. X article in 1947, George F. Kennan wrote that "the main element of any United States policy toward the Soviet Union must be that of a long term, patient but firm and vigilant containment of Russian expansive tendencies." I think it is reasonable to argue today, that the main aim of Americans should be to contain their own expansionist tendencies, and the proper way to do this is by redirecting national priorities toward the elimination of economic injustice at home.

One idea that has attracted the support of many former Volunteers is the proposal to internationalize the Peace Corps and thereby divorce it from U.S. foreign policy. I have seen no detailed analysis of this idea, only vague suggestions about putting the Peace Corps under an agency of the United Nations or of creating a separate international organization funded by host governments. Neither of these approaches seems to offer much promise at the moment. The U.N. does not have the funds nor the bureaucratic flexibility to handle a program like the Peace Corps, and the host governments cannot afford to gamble much money on an organization that delivers so little in apparent economic improvement.

It is, of course, difficult to prevent the United States government from dominating an international body. This is clearly what has happened already to the International Secretariat for Volunteer Service, a clearing house established in Washington in 1962 to coordinate Volunteer programs of other nations. The secretariat is funded by the participating governments with the United States contributing the largest amount. The Peace Corps details staff people to work in the ISVS office, and in 1966 claimed that the secretariat had helped 24 countries set up Volunteer programs. In a statement given to the Congress in 1966, the Peace Corps said that "U.S. participation in ISVS enables the United States to help provide technical assistance to countries where the provision of such assistance is in the United States' interest, but where *bilateral* provision of such assistance may not be possible." [10] It would be difficult to prevent the United States from using an international Peace Corps in the same way.

Another difficulty with an international volunteer organization would be its high vulnerability to infiltration by intelligence agencies. While it is doubtful that the Peace Corps is as pure as it pretends to be, the U.S. government does have the capability to minimize penetration. This would be much more difficult for an international organization, and even the suspicion of spy activity would make the organization unwelcome in the countries where it would be needed most.

But the most compelling argument against the international Peace Corps, in my opinion, is that it diverts attention from the more important problem of containing United States expansionism by reforming its internal political structure. It is the moral and political underdevelopment of the United States coupled with enormously destructive nuclear capability that demands the highest priority. To advance the development of the United States through economic and political reform may be the greatest service that young Americans can perform for the poor people of the third world, because it may be the only way to make sure that they will not ultimately become the victims of another Vietnam war.

It is against this background that one must consider what ought to be done with the Peace Corps. Is there some way whereby the overall impact on history of the organization can be altered so that it makes a greater contribution to peace and to the liquidation of poverty than it does to the expansion of American power? One approach may be worthy of exploration. Let us suppose that commentators like Hapgood and Bennett are correct and Volunteers are "getting a very special kind of education" as a result of their experience. Let us further assume that a significant number of them are being "radicalized" as some members of the CRV assert, and that "radicalization" means that they have learned that some fundamental political changes must be made in the United States if America's effort overseas is to benefit the poor and help avoid World War III. The logical thing to do then is to develop ways for returned Volunteers to "radicalize" the power potential of the middle classes by going into the white middle class ghettoes and educating the average Americans whose ignorance and confusion sustain the worst evils of the existing system.

Perhaps there is still a chance to turn what has been an instrument of American expansionism into a genuine movement for fundamental change in the American polity. To do this the Peace Corps would have to change its emphasis toward maximizing the educational and "radicalizing" impact on Volunteers. The purpose of volunteer service then would not be primarily to render aid to the economies of developing countries, although they might incidentally derive some minor benefits. The main object would be to build a corps of young people who would study the problems of poverty on an international scale, who would identify the impediments to change, who would develop ideas for improvement, and who in the process would acquire the knowledge and experience that would give them credibility when they returned home to educate their countrymen. In any case, it is the educational work at home *after* foreign service that should be the most important, and the Peace Corps itself should turn its attention to ways to do this. The effort should be organized, and the Volunteer should remain on salary.

It is obvious that such a scheme would meet with formidable resistance in the Congress from those forces who have a vested interest in preventing fundamental change. Such forces must be fought, and the Peace Corps, with over 25,000 returned Volunteers as of 1968, is not without manpower and talent to fight them. Of course, one must face the possibility that the fight would be lost. But it would be better for the Peace Corps to go out of existence than for it to continue to serve the interests of the rich at the expense of the poor. On the other hand, the fight might be won. There are signs that the American people are developing a greater awareness of the dangers of an expansionist foreign policy. There was no great public outcry against President Nixon's decision not to retaliate when the North Koreans shot down an American EC-121 spy plane. Even the frequently jingoistic *Time* magazine headed its story on the incident: "A New Lesson in the Limits of Power." Vietnam may have taught Americans a lesson that will open their minds to new ideas, to new ways of thinking about the rich and the poor nations. They may also be ready to consider new ways of dealing with the problems of poverty at home.

If this is true, then the first step is to begin some radical rethinking about ends and means within the Peace Corps and among the returned Volunteers. It is perhaps time for another conference like that held for returnees in 1965. It should probably not be held in Washington and the Peace Corps should probably not sponsor it, although it should participate and cooperate fully. Its purpose should be to develop mechanisms to turn the talents and energies of the Volunteers and returnees toward bringing about fundamental political and economic change in the United States.

Whether there is a conference or not, it is clear that the Peace Corps should not be allowed to continue business as usual. If the war in Vietnam can be finally liquidated, if the Peace Corps can demonstrate its own capability for radical change, then it will deserve additional support from idealistic young people. If, on the other hand, it is content to evolve as the colonial civil service of imperial America, as it already is in Micronesia, then people of conscience and idealism ought to have nothing to do with it, liberal congressmen ought to try to vote it out of existence, and if it survives it ought to be labeled and quarantined as the preserve of those who see it primarily as a vehicle for becoming, as its advertising promised, the future presidents of "U.S. Copper."

REFERENCES

CHAPTER I

1. See, for example: Juan Jose Arevalo, *The Shark and the Sardines* (New York: Lyle Stuart, 1961); Richard Barnet, *Intervention and Revolution* (New York: World, 1968); Amaury de Riencourt, *The American Empire* (New York: Dial, 1968); Robert Engler, *The Politics of Oil* (New York: Macmillan, 1961); Andre Gunder Frank, *Capitalism and Underdevelopment in Latin America* (New York: Monthly Review, 1969); J. William Fulbright, *The Arrogance of Power* (New York: Vintage, 1967); Keith Griffin, *Underdevelopment in Spanish America* (London: Allen and Unwin, 1969); David Horowitz, *The Free World Colossus* (London: Macgibbon and Kee, 1965); Claude Julien, *L'Empire Americain* (Paris: Grasset, 1968); Harry Magdoff, *The Age of Imperialism: The Economics of U.S. Foreign Policy* (New York: Monthly Review, 1969); James McMillan and Bernard Harris, *The American Take-Over of Britain* (New York: Hart, 1968): Raymond Mikesell, *U.S. Private and Government Investment Abroad* (Eugene, Ore.: University of Oregon, 1962); Kwame Nkrumah, *Neo-Colonialism, The Last Stage of Imperialism* (London: Nelson, 1965); George Liska, *Imperial America: The International Politics of Primacy* (Baltimore: Johns Hopkins Univ., 1967); Carl Oglesby and Richard Shaull, *Containment and Change* (New York: Macmillan, 1967); J. J. Servan-Schreiber, *The American Challenge* (New York: Atheneum, 1968); Ronald Steel, *Pax Americana* (New York: Viking, 1967).

CHAPTER II

1. J. A. Hobson, *Imperialism* (London: Allen and Unwin, 1938); V. I. Lenin, *Imperialism, The Highest Stage of Capitalism* (New York: International Publishers, 1939). The inadequacy of the Hobson-Lenin theories as explanations for all contemporary imperialist phenomena does not make them less important as continuing stimuli of political debate. See, for example, the special issue on imperialism of the French review, *Esprit* (April, 1969) with articles by Henri Denis, Celso Furtado, Stanley Hoffman, Pierre Hassner and others.

2. U.S. Congress, Senate Foreign Relations Committee. *Nomination of Lincoln Gordon to be Assistant Secretary of State for Inter-American Affairs.* Hearings, 89th Cong., 2nd Sess. (Feb. 1966), pp. 22-23.

3. See Jay Walz, "Report of Canadian Economists Asks Curbs on U.S. Concerns," *New York Times*, February 16, 1968; and Peter C.

Newman, "Backstage in One More American Takeover," *Macleans* (December 14, 1963), p. 17.

4. *New York Times*, February 7, 1968.

5. U.S. Congress, House Subcommittee on Foreign Economic Policy. *Involvement of U.S. Private Enterprise in Developing Countries*. Report, 90th Cong., 2nd Sess. (April 1968) (Washington: GPO, 1968), p. 3.

6. U.S. Congress, House Committee on Foreign Affairs, Subcommittee on Foreign Economic Policy. *The Involvement of U.S. Private Enterprise in Developing Countries*. Hearings, 90th Cong., 1st Sess. (Aug. 1967) (Washington: GPO, 1967), p. 76.

7. *International Herald Tribune*, Paris, March 26, 1969.

8. J. J. Servan-Schreiber, *The American Challenge* (New York: Atheneum, 1968).

9. The full text of Arnold's speech may be found in *The International Lawyer* (July 1967), pp. 534-547.

10. Irving Kristol, "We Can't Resign as 'Policeman of the World'," *New York Times Magazine* (May 12, 1968), p. 25.

CHAPTER III

1. A good description of this process was given by Edmund Burke in his speech of impeachment against Warren Hastings in 1788. It is reprinted in part in Ross Hoffman and Paul Levack, editors, *Burke's Politics, Selected Writings and Speeches of Edmund Burke* (New York: Knopf, 1949), pp. 234-236.

2. George Otto Trevelyan, *The Life and Letters of Lord Macaulay* (London: Longmans, Green, 1889), p. 396.

3. A. B. Keith, *Speeches and Documents on Indian Policy* (London: Oxford, 1922), p. 234.

4. *Ibid.*, p. 260-261.   5. *Ibid.*, p. 263-264.   6. *Ibid.*, p. 265.

7. Nearly the complete text of the minute is reprinted in George O. Trevelyan, *The Competition Wallah* (London: Macmillan, 1864), pp. 410-424. This quotation is from p. 422.

8. Quoted in Eric Stokes, *The English Utilitarians in India* (Oxford: Oxford, 1959), pp. 43-44.

9. Quoted in Stokes, *op. cit.* pp. 46-47.

10. *Peace Corps Volunteer* (March, 1963), p. 11.

CHAPTER IV

1. Harris Wofford, "The Future of the Peace Corps," *The Annals* (May, 1966), p. 144.

2. For background on the impact of *The Ugly American* see Thomas Wilson, Jr., "The Easy Chair," *Harper's* (June, 1959);

Donn V. Hart, "Overseas Americans in Southeast Asia: Fact in Fiction," *Far Eastern Survey* (Jan. 1961), pp. 1-16; and the debate in the U.S. Senate, *Congressional Record*, May 19, 1959, September 7, 1959. For an insightful view from an ex-Peace Corps Volunteer see Steve Clapp, "A Strangely Familiar Ghost," *Peace Corps Volunteer* (June 1968), p. 12.

3. William Lederer and Eugene Burdick, *The Ugly American* (New York: Fawcett [Crest], 1960), p. 225.

4. *New York Times*, November 3, 1960.

5. Jack Vaughn, *To Peace, With Love* (An Address by the Director of the Peace Corps) (Washington: Peace Corps, 1966), p. 10.

6. U.S. Congress, Senate Foreign Relations Committee. *Peace Corps Act Amendment of 1968, Hearings,* 90th Cong., 2nd Eess (April 1968) (Washington: GPO, 1968), p. 23.

7. *Congressional Record*, August 23, 1961. In his February 28, 1961 report to the President which recommended the immediate establishment of the Peace Corps, Sargent Shriver said: "The Peace Corps should take its place as a basic component of our whole overseas program." *Peace Corps Fact Book* (Washington: Peace Corps, 1961), p. 16.

8. U.S. Congress, House Foreign Affairs Committee. *Peace Corps Act Amendments*, Hearings, 87th Cong., 2nd Sess. (March 1962) (Washington: GPO, 1962), pp. 100-101.

9. U.S. Congress, House Appropriations Committee. *Foreign Operations Appropriations for 1962*, Hearings, 87th Cong., 1st Sess. (Aug. 1961) (Washington: GPO), 1961), p. 2.

10. U.S. Congress, House Appropriations Subcommittee on Foreign Operations, *Foreign Assistance and Related Appropriations for 1967*, Hearings, 89th Cong., 2nd Sess. (May 1966) (Washington: GPO, 1966), p. 474.

11. Arnold Zeitlin, *To the Peace Corps With Love* (New York: Doubleday, 1965), p. 342.

12. Quoted in Velma Adams, *The Peace Corps in Action* (Chicago: Follett, 1964), p. 93.

13. Frederic C. Thomas, "The Peace Corps in Morocco," *Middle East Journal* (Summer 1965), p. 281.

14. *Congressional Record*, August 23, 1961.

15. U.S. Congress, House Foreign Affairs Committee. *To Amend Further the Peace Corps Act*, Hearings, 88th Cong., 2nd Sess. (Jan., Feb. 1964), p. 46.

16. U.S. Congress, House Foreign Affairs Committee. *To Amend the Peace Corps Act*, Hearings, 88th Cong., 1st Sess. (Oct. 1963) (Washington: GPO, 1963), p. 64.

17. Jack Vaughn, *op. cit.*, p. 8.

CHAPTER V

1. "Some Facts and Figures," *Peace Corps Volunteer* (Dec. 1967), p. 19.

2. Henry Norman, "The Blue-Collar Volunteer," *Peace Corps Volunteer* (Dec. 1967), p. 13.

3. Michael J. Furst, "Rural Jobs and Skills for Generalists," *Peace Corps Volunteer* (March 1968), p. 13. The measurement of both development and impact is a matter of controversy among social scientists, and the data available about the Peace Corps is still limited. An interesting attempt by social scientists to measure Peace Corps impact is the Cornell study of villages in Peru: U.S. Peace Corps, *Measurement of Peace Corps Program Impact in the Peruvian Andes* (Ithaca: Cornell University, 1963).

4. *New York Times*, June 24, 1968.

5. "The Peace Corps on Campus," *Peace Corps Volunteer* (June 1968), pp. 4-8.

6. See Kingston Berlew, "Are We Getting 'Bland' Volunteers?" *Peace Corps Volunteer* (Dec. 1964), p. 2.

7. See this ad and a description of advertising policy in Linda Miller, "What's in it for me?" *Peace Corps Volunteer* (April 1967), pp. 12-13. Advertising policy is also discussed in *Ibid.* (Dec. 1965).

8. U.S. Congress, House Appropriations Committee, Subcommittee on Foreign Operations. *Foreign Operations Appropriations* Hearings, 87th Cong., 1st Sess. (Aug. 1961) (Washington: GPO, 1961), pp. 6-7.

9. *Ibid.*, p. 77.

10. U.S. Congress, House Appropriations Committee., Subcommittee on Foreign Operations. *Foreign Operations Appropriations for 1964.* Hearings, 88th Cong., 1st Sess. (April 1963) (Washington: GPO, 1963), p. 175.

11. *Ibid.*, pp. 175-176. See also *Peace Corps 1st Annual Report to Congress*, which says: "Extraordinary pressures were brought to bear on the Peace Corps to summarily drop Mr. Kamen" because he had "allegedly applauded the House Un-American Activities film 'Operation Abolition' in the wrong places. . . ." The report implies that Shriver resisted those pressures but makes no mention of the fact that Kamen was actually dismissed.

12. U.S. Congress, Senate Committee on Foreign Relations. *Peace Corps Act Amendment of 1968.* Hearings, 90th Cong., 2nd Sess. (April 1968) (Washington: GPO), 1968, p. 47.

13. *Ibid.*, p. 45.   14. *New York Times*, October 20, 1965.

15. *New York Times*, November 1, 1965.   16. *Ibid.*

17. Edwin Henry states: "The Selection Division of the Peace Corps favored highly intensive 'stress type' training programs." "Selection of Volunteers," *Annals* (May 1966), p. 34n.

18. For a critique of this facet of training see: George M. Guthrie, "Cultural Preparation for the Philippines," in Robert Textor (ed.), *Cultural Frontiers of the Peace Corps* (Cambridge: M.I.T. Press, 1966), p. 23. Jack Vaughn said on February 13, 1968: "We have considerably abated the rigors of our physical training program, whose importance we overestimated at the beginning."

19. *"Peace Corps Volunteer* (Oct. 1965), p. 27. For a perceptive, but rather cocky, description of what appears to be a fairly typical training program, see Alan Weiss, *High Risk/High Gain* (New York: St. Martin's, 1968).

20. Gene Gordon, *Finding Your Own Thing* (Washington: Peace Corps, 1968), pp. 7-8. For a different view on motivation see Grant Doe, "Volunteers as Agents for Development," *Peace Corps Volunteer* (Aug. 1967), p. 11.

21. Gene Gordon, *op. cit.*, p. 2.

22. U.S. Peace Corps, *Measurement of Peace Corps Program Impact in the Peruvian Andes* (Ithaca: Cornell University, 1963).

CHAPTER VI

1. Quoted in Harris Wofford, "The Future of the Peace Corps," *Annals* (May, 1966) p. 136.

2. Quoted in L.S.S. O'Malley, *The Indian Civil Service, 1601-1930* (London: John Murray, 1931) p. 180.

3. *Ibid.*   4. *Ibid.*, pp. 185-186.

5. Micronesia is discussed in greater in Chapter VII.

6. Robert Evans, "Wanted: PCV Decision Makers," *Peace Corps Volunteer* (June, 1967) p. 16.

7. U.S. Congress. House Appropriations Committee. *Foreign Assistance and Related Agencies Appropriations for 1969,* Hearings 90th Cong. 2nd sess. (June, 1968) (Washington: GPO, 1968) pp. 837, 858.

8. Quoted in Kirby Jones, "The Peace Corps Volunteer in the Field: Community Development," *Annals* (May, 1966) p. 64.

9. U.S. Congress. House, Committee on Foreign Affairs. Subcommittee on Inter-American Affairs. *Communism in Latin America,* Hearings (89th Cong. 1st Session) (March, 1965) pp. 89-91. The indication, "[security deletion]", appears in the original.

10. *Citizen in a Time of Change: The Returned Peace Corps Volunteer* (Washington: Peace Corps, 1965) p. 61.

11. U.S. Congress. House Committee on Foreign Affairs. Subcommittee on Inter-American Affairs. *Peace Corps Activities in Latin America and the Caribbean,* Hearings. 89th Cong. 1st Sess. (October, 1965) p. 12.

12. *Ibid.*, pp. 13-14.

13. See U.S. Congress. House. Appropriations Committee. *For-*

eign Assistance and Related Agencies Appropriations for 1969, p. 432.

14. *Ibid.* In the early days of the Peace Corps, Volunteers who resigned before the end of their tour were required to pay for their own return transportation. Ex-Volunteers talk of various strategems designed to get the government to pay for transportation in early terminations, among them writing a letter to the CIA. Some CIA contacts may be nothing more than devices of this sort.

15. U.S. Congress. House, Foreign Affairs Committee. *To Amend Further the Peace Corps Act,* Hearings. 88th Cong. 2nd Sess. (January-February, 1964) (Washington: GPO, 1964) p. 62.

16. U.S. Air Force. *U.S. Air Force Fact Sheet 68-14* (Washington: Air Force, 1968).

17. Robert P. Everett, "Sick Call at Ban Chieng Yeun," *The Airman* (January, 1968), p. 22.

18. Joe T. Williams and Thomas P. Griffin, "Military Veterinarians in Civic Action Programs," *Digest* (August, 1967) p. 6. See also: "The Air Commandos: Preventive Medicine," *Time* (July 26, 1968) p. 37.

CHAPTER VII

1. U.S. Congress. Joint Committee on Atomic Energy. Special Subcommittee on Radiation, *Biological and Environmental Effects of Nuclear War,* Hearings, 86th Cong. 1st Sess. (June, 1959) (Washington; USGPO, 1959), p. 394.

2. United Nations. Trusteeship Council. Official Records. *Report of the United Nations Visiting Mission to the Trust Territory of the Pacific Islands, 1961,* T/1582, Supplement No. 2 (New York: United Nations, 1961), p. 34.

3. *New York Times,* July 3, 1968.

4. United Nations. Trusteeship Council. Official Records. *Report of the United Nations Visiting Mission to the Trust Territory of the Pacific Islands, 1964,* T/1628 (New York: United Nations, 1964), p. 3.

5. United Nations. Trusteeship Council. Official Records. *Report of the World Health Organization on its Investigation of Complaints Contained in a Petition Concerning the Trust Territory of the Pacific Islands,* T/1647 (New York: United Nations, 1966), p. 12.

6. *Ibid.,* pp. 5, 6.   7. *Ibid.,* p. 11.

8. *Congressional Record,* October 15, 1968. For clarity, I have edited apparent errors in punctuation.

9. U.S. Congress. Senate. Committee on Foreign Relations. *Peace Corps Act Amendment of 1967,* Hearings, 90th Congress, 1st Sess. (May, 1967) (Washington: USGPO, 1967) p. 27.

10. The training syllabus for the Micronesia VII teams which trained in the summer of 1968 says: "To Peace Corps in Micronesia

[involvement] means a spirit of kinship with the Micronesian people. To care, as they care, for what they care about. It is sharing, born of a spiritual and intellectual curiosity (the two are not incompatible); a sharing which becomes an involvement in any aspect of going activity which gets you to belong, in a more meaningful way, with the people engaged in that activity . . . The ends are changes in attitude, including yours. Your actions, to have force, must reflect the thinking of the people; must be what they want. As you become a part of the activities, your needs become part of those of the people. You become a meaningful factor in the direction that community activity takes, and while you are not here to steer a community in any given direction you are, through involvement and acceptance by the community, in a position to channel activity in a positive direction, increasing the impact on the traditional barriers to change." *Peace Corps Training; Micronesia VII* (n. p. : n. d. [Washington: Peace Corps, 1968]), p. 1.

11. United Nations. Trusteeship Council. Official Records. *Report of the United Nations Visiting Mission to the Trust Territory of the Pacific Islands, 1967* (New York: United Nations, 1967) p. 43.

12. *Peace Corps in Micronesia,* Briefing Paper (Washington: Peace Corps, 1968), p. 8.

13. *Peace Corps Training; Micronesia* VII, p. 31.

14. *Peace Corps in Micronesia,* p. 6.

15. Stella Margold, "Liberia—Open Door Policy Invites Foreign Capital," *International Trade Review* (July, 1964), p. 12.

16. Such labor practices when found in Communist countries are often referred to as "slave labor" by American publicists. In Liberia it is referred to as an "arrangement" with local chiefs who handle the impressment. See Russell U. McLaughlin, *Foreign Investment and Development in Liberia* (New York: Praegar, 1966) pp. 92ff for an uncritical account.

17. "A Second Look at Liberia," *Africa Report,* (October, 1966), p. 24.

18. Stella Margold, *op. cit.,* p. 13.

19. See J. Gus Liebenow, "Liberia," in Gwendolen M. Carter, *African One-Party States* (Ithaca: Cornell Univ. Press, 1962) pp. 368ff.

20. Fletcher Knebel, *The Zin-Zin Road* (New York: Bantam, 1967).

21. *The Peace Corps in Ethiopia* (Washington: Peace Corps, 1968), p. 2.

22. *Ibid.,* p. 3.   23. *Ibid.,* p. 6.

24. Peace Corps Ethiopia, Form letter to invitees dated April 2, 1968, signed by David E. Berlew.

25. *International Herald Tribune* (Paris), March 29-30, 1969.

CHAPTER VIII

1. *Forum Peace Corps India December 1967* (New Delhi: Peace Corps, 1967) p. 31.
2. *New York Times,* June 14, 1967.
3. Stuart Awbrey, "Politics and the Peace Corps," *Peace Corps Volunteer* (September, 1967) p. 3.
4. Lewis W. Wolfson, "The Peace Corps Volunteers and Freedom of Expression," *The Providence* (R.I.) *Journal,* July 23, 1967.
5. Bruce Murray in letter to Windmiller, Dec. 23, 1968.
6. *New York Times,* July 16, 1967.
7. *Peace Corps 6th Annual Report* (Washington: Peace Corps, 1968) p. 44.
8. *Citizen in a Time of Change: The Returned Peace Corps Volunteer* (Washington: Peace Corps, 1965) p. 13, 14.
9. *Ibid.,* p. 56.
10. For a description of early activities of the CRV see: Francis Pollock, "The New World They See," *The Nation* (July 3, 1967) pp. 15-17.
11. *Citizens in a Time of Change,* p. 41.
12. U.S. Congress. House. Appropriations Committee. *Foreign Assistance and Related Agencies Appropriations for 1969,* Hearings, 90th Cong. 2nd Sess. (June, 1968) (Washington: GPO, 1968) p. 416.

CHAPTER IX

1. U. S. Congress. Senate. Committee on Foreign Relations. *Peace Corps Act Amendments, 1969* Hearings. 91st Cong. 1st Sess. (June, 1969) (Washington: GPO, 1969) p. 2.
2. Joseph H. Blatchford, *The Peace Corps of the 1970's* (Washington: Peace Corps, 1969) p. 1.
3. U. S. Congress. Senate. Committee on Foreign Relations. *Peace Corps Act Amendments, 1969* Hearings. 91st Cong. 1st Sess. (June, 1969) (Washington: GPO, 1969) p. 44.

CHAPTER X

1. Symposium, "No More Vietnams?", *The Atlantic* (December, 1968), p. 101.
2. See especially G. William Domhoff, *Who Rules America?* (Englewood Cliffs: Spectrum, 1967).
3. *War/Peace Report* (October, 1968) p. 9.
4. Arthur Barber, "Emerging New Power: The World Corporation," *War/Peace Report* (October, 1968) p. 7.
5. George W. Ball, "Making World Corporations Into World

Citizens," *War/Peace Report* (October, 1968) p. 10.

6. See Stokely Carmichael and Charles V. Hamilton, *Black Power* (New York: Vintage, 1967), especially Chapter I; and Tom Hayden, "Colonialism and Liberation in America," *Viet Report* (Summer, 1968), pp. 32-39 ff.

7. *Peace Corps 1969; Editor's Background Information* (Washington: Peace Corps, 1968) p. 16. Other figures given:

Profit Organizations	1260
Non-Profit Organizations	629
State and Local Governments	368
War on Poverty	253
International Organizations and Foreign Governments	91
Other	134

8. U.S. Congress. House Committee on Foreign Affairs. Subcommittee on Foreign Economic Policy. *The Involvement of U.S. Private Enterprise in Developing Areas,* Hearings, 90th Cong. 1st Sess. (August, 1967) (Washinington: GPO, 1968), p. 81.

9. U.S. Congress. Senate. Foreign Relations Committee. *Nomination of Jack Hood Vaughn to be Director of the Peace Corps,* Hearing, 89th Cong. 2nd Sess. (February, 1966), (Washington: GPO, 1966), p. 25.

10. U.S. Congress. House. Committee on Foreign Affairs. *Peace Corps Amendments of 1966 (Fiscal Year 1967),* Hearings, 89th Cong. 2nd Sess. (July, 1966) (Washington: GPO, 1966), p. 34.